A JOURNEY TO MORIAH

To Bob & Mary,
Blessings!
Rhea Murray

International Standard Book Number:
0-9667237-0-8

Library of Congress Catalogue Card Number:
98-87829

Printed in the United States of America

For information contact:
Banta & Pool Literary Properties, LLC
1020 Greenwood Avenue
Bloomington, Indiana 47401

e-mail: writerpool@aol.com

This book is dedicated to Butch, my beloved husband. I could never have climbed so high without the safety net of your love.

I would like to thank the following people without whose support this book could never have become a reality: Frank Banta, Marc Griffin, Rob Banaszak (my personal angel), Dixie Beer, and Nancy Elliot.

I also want to take this opportunity to thank my editor, Gary Pool. I treasure the journey we took together to write my story. Thank you for never flinching when I gave you my rawest truths. Thank you for your belief in me and my story, and thank you for all those kleenexes. How blessed I am to call you friend at journey's end.

— Rhea Murray

A Journey to Moriah

by
Rhea Murray

with Gary Pool

Published by
Banta & Pool, LLC
Bloomington, Indiana

This is a true story. The characters are real people. In the interest of privacy, however, some of their names have been changed. The general setting is southern Indiana, but the names of certain institutions and geographical locations have also been altered.

CHAPTER I

This little place, this cartographer's tittle, has been my home all my life and, strange as it seems to me today, up until a very few years ago it practically comprised the entire world as I knew it. I was born in 1950 and grew up, along with my younger brother, in the poorest neighborhood of Sunnyside, a town, in those days, of 9,632 souls in southern Indiana (the population has since doubled). Poverty forced both my parents to give up school after completing only the sixth grade, and find whatever work they could. We lived a hard-scrabble life and, despite my dad's long hours of manual labor, often did not have enough money to make ends meet. Eventually, when I was about ten years old, my father did receive training as a millwright. He was then able to find a better factory job. After that our standard of living began to improve somewhat. At least we had enough to eat from then on, and were finally able to move from our tiny rented place into a four-room house that my parents could afford to buy.

From a very early age I became closely acquainted with the ridicule, humiliation and awful, debilitating pain humans are capable of inflicting upon one of their number who happens to be different from the rest. Because of a birth defect, complicated by a childhood accident, my mother was left without the bridge of her nose. But she was by no means unattractive, being possessed of a wonderful, sweet smile, beautiful violet-blue eyes and a kindly disposition. Still, in public people would usually stare and sometimes mock and laugh at her. Even in church, children, whose parents no doubt considered them precious darlings, made faces and called her "pig nose." As a result, mother came to view herself as grossly disfigured and offensive to look upon, and somehow oddly deserving of the cruel treatment she received from many of our neighbors and fellow Christians. Gradually she withdrew from the meager society of Sunnyside, often refusing even to leave the house for many days at a time. As a child, I would sometimes hear her crying behind the door of her bedroom, and sadly wonder why it was necessary for her to suffer so ignominiously. No one had the right to do this to her. But mother, being a woman of her generation, and also very gentle and docile by nature, did not know how to fight back. She simply accepted humiliation as her lot in life, almost like some punishment she deserved just for having been born.

Owing to my mother's self-imposed isolation, as a family, we pretty much kept to ourselves, venturing from home usually only when necessary and hardly ever having visitors. We did not own a car, and for many years (until my father was able to get his better job) we also didn't have a telephone in the house, poverty making these quite common things seem to us like great luxuries. This fairly reclusive life meant that when I started school I had developed few of the social skills necessary to relate to the other children. Making friends did not come easily, and I was often very lonely.

One of our few regular excursions into the outside world was to attend church. We became members of a local fundamentalist Church Of The Nazarene as a result, oddly enough, of the death of my grandfather. His funeral had been held at the church and, since up to that point we had had no particular religious affiliation, my parents decided it was time for us to start attending services. For nine years thereafter we hardly missed a Sunday.

Then my mother became very ill. As the result of an operation that had gone seriously awry several years earlier (at which time an attempt had been made to correct her facial deformity using bone harvested from one of her hips) she often suffered long bouts of excruciating and immobilizing pain. During one of these extended illnesses we resumed our more or less sequestered way of life. Because she was wheelchair bound, she could neither work nor take care of the house. Since we did not wish to go to church without her, we simply opted to stay home.

Throughout our long absence from church, however, no one from the congregation ever came to call nor did the pastor inquire as to why we had stopped attending services. Of course nothing was ever said, so I can never be certain of the exact reason for this, but I suspect poverty played a big role in our virtual invisibility. After all, we didn't have a car or nice clothes and could never afford to put much, if anything, into the collection plate. Our lack of money and material possessions meant we didn't count. So, like poor folks throughout history, we were simply, and very conveniently, ignored. This self-imposed ignorance eases the troubled conscience of the more fortunate, and it doesn't cost them anything.

Then Red and Blue Sunday rolled around. The church was divided up into two teams, the red and the blue. The idea was to see which team could bring the most people to church on the appointed Sunday. The losing team would then have to prepare a steak dinner for the winners. Suddenly we were receiving visits from members of the two teams, who begged us to attend church in their behalf on Red and Blue Sunday. That was the only time during my mother's illness that we were ever visited by members of that church. Obviously, we were nothing more to those people than warm bodies to be dragged out of cold storage when they needed us, but otherwise to be forgotten, conveniently unnoticeable. We did not go to church on Red and Blue Sunday, despite the pleading of the members of the two teams. In fact, we never attended that church again.

Childhood was anything but a validating experience for me, as is often the case for poor kids. My parents were among the emotional and psychological walking-wounded, refugees of a generation born in the iron grip of the Great Depression and then passed over inexplicably by economic recovery. Trapped by their unreconciled rage against the abuses they had suffered as children at the hands of their parents, and the dehumanizing social injustices of adult life, they could hardly affirm their own existence, let alone that of their children. For just as our family was invisible to the members of that little Nazarene Church, so I seemed to be invisible to my parents, though doubtless for quite different reasons. It was as if life itself had laid such terrible burdens upon them that they could not see past its struggles, failures and countless insurmountable hardships to the solitary place where their little girl was trying to figure out who she was and where she fit in. I have tasted of their rage, and I understand it. It is the bitter harvest of many generations of physical and mental abuse. It is the legacy of gall.

If life at home for me was lonely, it was sometimes also quite dangerous. My father had a darkly brutal side to his nature that could, at any moment, flare into terrifying violence. Once, when I was five, my brother and I were having a pillow fight. The noise from our play awakened my dad, who at the time was working a night shift. Angered at having his sleep interrupted, he spanked both my brother and me. My brother cried and cried until he noticed that I was not even whimpering. "Why aren't you crying?" he asked. "Why, because I'm not a big baby," I replied, perhaps a bit too smugly. My brother ran from the room. I heard the front door slam and a moment later my maniacally enraged father was standing over me with a branch from a rosebush, flailing away at my naked legs. "How dare you tell your brother that I didn't spank you as hard because I love you more than I do him!" he screamed. My frantic efforts to cover my legs with my hands only resulted in greater injury. For his own needy reasons, my brother had told a most terrible lie. Of course, I had not said any such thing, but my father would not let me explain. He would rather demonstrate by his actions that what he *thought* I had said was indeed false. He just kept beating me with that thorny switch until the blood flowed like water, turning the sheets of my bed dark crimson. I don't know how long this thrashing might have lasted, had my mother not finally intervened. The physical wounds would heal fairly quickly, the emotional ones, however, would require a lifetime.

My mother had made up her mind early on in their marriage that it was better, which is to say "safer," to swallow whatever my father dished out than to challenge him. She was often not in the best of health, either physically or emotionally, and she had no particularly marketable skills to provide her with the means to escape. In short, she was hopelessly trapped. But she laid a plan that she believed would save me from her fate and protect me from the frequent abuses of my father. Her strategy for my ultimate liberation involved marrying me off to the first available man who came along. So, when I was sixteen, with the well-meaning, if misguided, urging and legal consent of my mother, I married a young man who, in very short order, proved himself to be every bit as abusive and irascible as my father had been.

*
*   *

My first marriage lasted eight and a half years. Though my husband did mistreat me physically, choking me, on one occasion, until I fell unconscious, he also took particular delight in psychological abuse. On more than one occasion, for example, he would come into the bathroom while I was taking a bath and hold a plugged-in electric razor over the tub, taunting me with threats to drop it into the water. Toward the end of this ill-fated union, suicide was becoming an increasingly appealing option to me.

One of the few bright spots, on the otherwise terribly bleak landscape of those eight and a half years, was the wonderful baby girl who came into my life. Because my husband was thought to be sterile (later, after our divorce, this proved not to be the case as he did subsequently father a child by his second wife) we chose adoption. Tanya was only thirteen days old when we brought her home. I adored her, and she became my saving grace during the slow, but inevitable, disintegration of my marriage. She was what I lived for. I never thought of her as anything but my child, though I also considered it unfair for her not to know she was adopted. So, when the time eventually did come that she began asking questions, I told her the truth. There were repercussions from this later, when Tanya was a teenager, that I had not anticipated. Though I still believe it is important for adopted children to know they are adopted, looking back on it now I think I handled it rather badly by not allowing her to express her feelings, especially her anger, the way I should have. I thought I was listening, but in fact I wasn't, being more concerned with fixing everything, trying to be "supermom" rather than attempting honestly to understand my daughter's feelings and why she was expressing them as she was.

When I finally did leave my first husband, my daughter and I were homeless for three months. My mother, being very traditional in her views on marriage, and having been kept completely in the dark concerning the brutalization I had endured (marital abuse nearly always causes such shame for the victim in our society), told me flatly that my place was with my husband and I could not move back in with my parents. Tanya and I wandered from one motel room or dingy, one-room flat to the next until the wonderful man who would become my second husband took us in.

Like me, Butch was a child of acute poverty. Most young people of today would probably find it difficult to believe, but he grew up in a very primitive, two-room log cabin, with no running water, out in the country, far from the nearest tiny village. It became a standing joke, between Butch and me, that his family was better off than mine because they had an electric light in their outhouse and we did not.

Butch's father was an abusive alcoholic whose life had been thoroughly devastated by his military service during the Second World War in Europe. The horrors of that war haunted him until the day he shot himself to death in the presence of his wife when Butch was only seventeen. Now the terrible tragedy of that awful event continues to haunt, to this day, those he left behind.

Butch used to say that he and I were like two birds, each with one broken wing. Alone we were injured, earth-bound and joyless, but together we could soar, happy and free, beyond the clouds. He also believed that the terrible cycles of pain and abuse, which had ensnared our lives and the lives of our parents and their parents before them, must end with us.

Life began for me on the day I met Butch Murray. He's been my salvation, and I like to think I've been his as well. Nine months after my divorce from my first husband, on April 25th, 1976, Butch and I were married. I was twenty-five years old at the time.

CHAPTER

II

Impulsively, Butch and I decided to hold our wedding out-of-doors. This turned out not to be among the most brilliant decisions we have ever made. Southern Indiana is not known for its meteorological stability, and at no time of the year is this more the case than in the spring. The weather on April 24th was spectacularly beautiful, sunny, clear-skyed and warm. That night, however, the mercury plummeted thirty degrees in a matter of hours and the next day, just before the ceremony was to start, a bone-chilling drizzle began to fall.

Fifty shivering guests crowded into the little shelter house on top of Skyline View in the Clark State Forest. (We had chosen that location because, while homeless, I would sometimes climb to the top of the fire tower there. The sweeping, panoramic view of nature had a soothing, calming affect upon my confused and troubled spirit). To ward off the chill, at least to some extent, the men built a roaring fire in the stone fireplace inside the shelter house. The minister decided that standing before the fire would be a good place for us to exchange our vows. He stood with his back to the fire, and our guests crowded in closer for warmth and in order to hear better.

I wore a powder-blue, floor-length dress, daisies and ribbons adorning my hair. Butch was decked out in his powder-blue leisure suit and boldly mottled shirt. Fashion in the mid-seventies was not known for the tasteful discretion of its subtle understatement.

Marcia, my best friend, and soon-to-be sister-in-law, was matron of honor. Her husband served as best man.

Things were getting pretty cozy, with our friends and family gathered snugly around us before the crackling fire. Suddenly, in the midst of the proceedings, the minister, still with his back to the dancing flames, urgently whispered: "Please, back up! It's getting hot here." But the guests had not heard clearly what the pastor had said, so rather than retreating they crowded in closer upon us.

"Back up!" he reiterated, in an urgent whisper that was more like a shout. "It's getting very hot back here." And he began frantically fanning his backside with his hand, his face now quite crimson and beaded with sweat.

When the little crowd finally realized what was going on, they burst into a pandemonium of gleeful laughter that took a good five minutes to subside. Even then, Marcia found it impossible to bring her guffaws under control. Finally, I nudged her with my elbow. "Do you mind?" I said. "I'm trying my best to get married here." With considerable difficulty she managed to suppress her giggles, at least for the moment.

We tried to continue with the service, but when the next words out of the preacher's mouth were: "This is a beautiful day for a wedding," the guests dissolved into another tumult of good-natured laughter.

So, Butch and I were married in the midst of laughter and rain. And what, in fact, could have been more symbolically appropriate? For, as the minister eventually pointed out, when he was at last permitted to deliver his sermon, a marriage is the formal recognition of the union of two people whose fondest desire is to share with each other their joy and happiness as well as their tears and sorrow, until they are parted in death.

Even though Butch was kind and gentle and unwaveringly considerate of my feelings, I remember secretly fearing very early on in our marriage that this was the "honeymoon" stage and it wouldn't last. Such sweet tenderness was quite alien to my experience, and it took a while before I learned to trust it.

One evening, shortly after we were married, Butch took me out to dinner at quite a nice seafood restaurant in Bardstown, Kentucky. The portions were very lavish and, try as I might, I simply could not finish my meal.

"What's the matter, honey?" he asked, noticing I was troubled.

"I'm sorry," I hesitantly replied. "I just can't finish it."

"Why, Rhea," Butch said, touching my hand, deep concern in his eyes, "whatever makes you think you have to?"

Butch was unaware that in my first marriage one of the easiest ways of arousing my husband's ire was to be unable to finish a meal *he* had bought for me. This simple thing might unleash a virtual torrent of hateful, and meaningless, abuse.

I would ask Butch for his permission to go places or to make purchases. He gently informed me that he was not my father, that I was an adult and did not need to ask anyone's permission to leave our house. He did not view me as his property. His love was born of a deeply held confidence and faith in me.

Butch had but one earnest request, and that was that I allow people to see my green eyes. He used to say that when we first met, for a long time he didn't know how beautiful my eyes were because I always kept them downcast. Of course, this was a result of several long years of practice at trying to make myself as invisible as I could. But Butch would have none of that. He insisted I know and feel my own self-worth as a human being. This involved, among many other things, holding my head up and facing the world head-on, with dignity.

One autumnal Saturday afternoon he took me for a drive, and before I knew it we were parked in front of the showroom window of a music store. Through the glass I could see the many new pianos on display. Butch knew that one of my foremost wishes was to one day own a piano. I had told him how, from early childhood, I had been captivated watching people play in church.

"What are we doing here?" I asked, turning away from the window and regarding my new husband with some puzzlement.

Smiling warmly, he said: "We're here so you can pick out your new piano."

I was stunned. "But, how can we afford it? " I stammered, knowing full well that we couldn't.

"If we wait until we can afford it," Butch tenderly replied, "you may never have your piano at all. Don't worry, honey. We'll manage. Please, don't deny me this pleasure." He was almost pleading. I was dumbstruck.

After I had picked the piano of my dreams, Butch told the salesman he would purchase it only on condition that it be delivered that very day. "She's waited long enough," he said. Later in the afternoon, I stood in absolute amazement as that beautiful instrument was brought into our living room. I stayed near my new piano the rest of the day, not even wanting to leave the sight of it to go to bed.

Gradually, I began to trust my feelings about my husband and our life together. As a result, my self-confidence became stronger, and I began to grow as a person by leaps and bounds. Even though, being just as human as the rest of us, Butch is sometimes plagued by insecurities, he has never failed to encourage me every step of the way, despite whatever fears and misgivings he may have had about the perils and pitfalls of my course of action. He is always there to catch me should I stumble. I have come to realize that he really does place my needs, desires and well-being above his own. It is this selfless giving that is the essence of the real and living love with which he honors me.

I was elated when, for the first time in my life, I became pregnant. Butch too was completely overjoyed. I had longed for many years to experience the deep, almost mystical, sensation of nurturing a human life inside my body. A few weeks after learning of my pregnancy, however,

I began hemorrhaging. I was terrified. My doctor immediately hospitalized me, and we spent the next two weeks trying to save my baby. When it looked as though I was out of the woods, the doctor at last allowed me to go home. Unfortunately, a follow-up examination a few days later revealed that the fetus had succumbed in my womb. Emotionally devastated, I was readmitted to the hospital for a dilation and curettage procedure (more commonly known as scraping the womb).

Six months later I was hospitalized yet again with my second miscarriage. Utterly traumatized by a grief the profundity of which is impossible to describe to those who have not experienced it, I sat for hours on end, staring blankly at the wall of my hospital room. It was New Year's Eve. The next day I was scheduled for my second D & C procedure.

Suddenly, I was aroused from my stupor by a curious sound of tinkling glasses, as though someone were carrying them down the corridor toward my door. Like a little boy up to some mischief, Butch came stealing into my room, a bottle of champagne and two glasses hidden beneath his coat.

"I want to have a New Year's toast with my pretty wife," he said. "I know it's past visiting hours, but I got permission to see the new year in with you. You're only allowed to have one, though," Butch admonished with a gentle smile, as he poured the sparkling, golden liquid into my glass.

We drank our toast, and Butch held me in his arms and kissed away my tears with great tenderness. "I know the year ahead is starting out on a really rotten note," he said softly. "But it'll turn out all right. You'll see."

"What makes you so sure?" I asked him, gloomily.

"Why, because we still have each other," was his confident reply.

A few weeks after my release from the hospital, Marcia announced that she was pregnant. A short time later, she asked me to go shopping with her in preparation for her new arrival. I followed her from one store to the next as she enthusiastically sought out just the right clothes, bedding and playthings for her baby. She was so very happy. All at once she stopped dead in her tracks and turned to face me. "Oh, Rhea!" she said, putting down her parcels and taking my face in her cupped hands. "How thoughtless of me not to realize until now how terribly painful this must be for you!" Her eyes were filled with compassion and understanding. "How I love you for being here with me," she whispered. "I know how dearly it must have cost you."

I adored Marcia. When I introduced her to someone, I always stated proudly that she was my very best friend, who also just happened to be my sister-in-law. As I looked into her beautiful and deeply sympathetic eyes that afternoon, I could not imagine that anything ever could come between us. Years later I would learn most painfully how dreadfully wrong I had been.

Three weeks following the birth of Marcia's son, Jason, I learned that I was once again pregnant. I was too afraid to hope, being not at all sure I could withstand the emotional shock of another miscarriage.

In my fifth month I started to spot. I was rushed to emergency and once again admitted to the hospital. It was impossible for me to interact with the staff or any of my visitors. I had simply shut down emotionally. Well-meaning people sometimes say the most insensitive things to a woman who experiences a miscarriage, such as: "It was God's will," or "You will have others," or, even worse, "It wouldn't have been right, anyway." I simply couldn't put up with any more of those remarks while I was desperately trying to save my unborn baby's life. Even Butch kept silent. The room was like a sepulchre, with mummified versions of my friends and family lined up in stony silence along the walls.

Then a strange thing happened. A person I did not recognize paid me a visit. This stranger was carrying a ceramic figurine of praying hands. She crossed the room and placed the figurine on the nightstand beside my bed. She smiled kindly, patted my folded hands and departed just a mysteriously as she had entered, without uttering a single word.

I picked up the figurine. Wrapped about it was a newspaper article by Ann Landers about how, when we struggle with sorrow and despair, God suffers with us. It is never the will of God that we should suffer, the article declared. It was a personal message directed at me, and I knew it in my soul. God did not want me to endure the loss of yet another child. He was with me. At the bottom of the clipping was a note indicating that the woman who had delivered this remarkable gift had been my roommate when I was hospitalized with my second miscarriage. She was God's messenger.

After returning home, however, it seemed that each passing day brought renewed anxiety over my pregnancy. I was becoming obsessed by the fear of losing my baby. One night, during this time, I had a startlingly vivid dream. I could see the child I was carrying within my body. It was a beautiful baby boy. He smiled reassuringly at me and waved his little hand. "Don't worry, mom," he said. "I'll be okay." When I awoke from that dream I knew with absolute certainty my child would be a boy. In addition, I felt calm, almost serene, and possessed of a new sense of confidence. From that point on, I was able to fully enjoy my pregnancy.

In the spring of 1978, with my due date rapidly approaching, I became concerned about my daughter, Tanya. How would she feel about having a brother who was not adopted as she had been? She was five years old at the time, and full of many questions. I was trying to decide whether I should breast feed or bottle feed the new baby. So, I asked Tanya what she thought. She wanted to know which she had been. When I told her that she had been bottle fed, she declared that her new sibling should be as well. My decision to honor that request was a good one. In so doing, I involved Tanya more closely with the process of having a new baby and all the changes that this event would bring to the life of our family. It helped her to adjust by preventing her from becoming alienated. It also helped her to feel closer to her baby brother.

My delivery date came and went without result. We waited and waited until finally my doctor decided it would be necessary to induce labor. Once again I was admitted to the hospital and at 8:00 AM my labor began. Butch and I spent hours walking up and down the halls in an effort to try and make my contractions stronger. Then we would play two-handed solitaire to pass the time. The minutes turned into hours and the hours into days. Finally, at 6:00, on the evening of May 2nd, the doctor broke my water and I got down to some very serious child-birthing. My labor intensified. The baby was in the wrong position. He was pressing against my tailbone causing me excruciating pain with every contraction. I just kept concentrating on the thought that my child would soon be in my arms, and that seemed to alleviate the pain. Finally, at 10:18 PM, our baby boy was born. After Butch saw me safely back to my room, I encouraged him to go home and get some rest. He had been with me every second of my labor and delivery. I really think he had worked about as hard as I had. He looked exhausted.

We named our baby Bruce, after Butch's closest army buddy in Vietnam. They had met at the U.S. Army Induction Center in Indianapolis in 1967 and gone through basic training together at Fort Knox. Both were assigned to mechanical training school in Aberdeen, Maryland, and both went to Vietnam. Though the army seeks to discourage the formation of such close bonds between soldiers in time of war, the two men stayed good friends throughout their tour of duty and remain so even today.

Because of my difficult delivery, I was under strictest instructions from my doctor and the nurses to stay in bed. They wanted me to remain flat on my back for at least twelve hours following the birth. In the middle of the night, however, I managed to sneak from my room and visit the nursery to have another peek at my sweet boy. Oh, the delicious joy I felt, gazing down at my son. God had used me to bring this new life into the world. I was thrilled beyond words. I felt as though I could surely fly.

The next day, when my husband came to visit me, he told me to look outside. There on the sidewalk stood my beautiful, brown-eyed, button-nosed daughter holding my mother's hand. Tanya waved to me and blew me kisses. Unfortunately, it was the hospital's policy not to allow children younger than a certain age onto the wards. Watching her from my window, all I wanted was to get out of that hospital so we could start being a family again.

CHAPTER

Bruce was such a good-natured baby. He seldom cried and always seemed eager to present us with that big, winsome smile of his. As a toddler, he was very animated and his antics kept us in stitches for hours.

Seeing the way my husband took care of his new son was a truly heart-warming experience. Each time I watched him give Bruce a bath, or feed him, or even change his diaper, a rush of pure joy would wash over me, sometimes bringing with it tears and emotion so intense I would have to leave the room. I felt from the very beginning, almost instinctively, that Butch would be an involved and loving parent. This early feeling of mine has always proved to be correct. Even in infanthood, Bruce developed a close, loving relationship with his father. This strong bond between father and son would prove to be of crucial importance to them both in later years. Tanya, who was five years old when Bruce was born, also loved her little brother very much and, especially when he was a tiny newborn, was extremely protective toward him.

I wanted nothing short of the perfect childhood for my kids, one totally different from what I had had. I really did want to be that June Cleaver/Harriet Nelson kind of mother so ubiquitous on the TV sitcoms of the fifties and sixties. As trite and clichéd as that seems, even to me, today, these larger-than-life, television-land moms embodied all my ideals of what the consummate mother should be. They were the models I held up before myself, and their make-believe families were the models for my real-life family as well. To me, it was all just part of the American dream. I was too captivated by the very fantasy itself to recognize the contrived shallowness of its distorted perspective on life.

Butch had two children from a previous marriage, Mike and Lora. We had visitation rights every other weekend. It seemed to me only natural to include them in the perfect world of my "TV" family. Butch and I would plan picnics, or take the kids to amusement parks, boating, on camping trips, or go-carting. You name it, and if it was a "family" type thing, we did it. I cooked elaborate meals and often baked brownies, the children's favorite treat. Frequently I would also include my baby sister, Kathy, who was only a couple of years older than my daughter, in our family and outings.

We found ourselves a tidy little Presbyterian Church out in the country. It was very unlike the church where I had grown up, none of that hellfire and brimstone business here. Sundays, we would pack up the kids in the car and head out to church, always anticipating the dip in the road that would leave us momentarily airborne and tickle our tummies on the way down. The car was filled with laughter, and at Sunday School, when the teacher asked Tanya what she liked best about coming to church, she replied, without hesitation, "The big bump in the road."

On December 23, 1979, Bruce was baptized while being held in his father's arms. Butch was baptized at the same time. My husband's father, having been an atheist, had not exactly encouraged his children to attend church, let alone partake of its sacraments. To watch my son and his father being baptized together was one of the many supremely beautiful high points of my life. It was amazing how every component, every little jigsawed piece of my new fairy-tale existence was falling, with such seemingly effortless perfection, into place. I couldn't have been more blissfully happy.

Lora was about ten years old when Bruce was born. She had her father's striking, sky-blue eyes, eyes that could often reveal so much of what was going on behind them without her uttering a word. I began to notice hints of anger and bitterness in Lora. Naively, it had never occurred to me that she might have wanted her father all to herself, on those weekend visits, instead of our being just one big, happy family. Gradually, she began to find more and more excuses not to come with us. Butch tried, with increasing frustration, to reach her, but she only withdrew further and further from him and from us as a family. Tensions were developing between Butch and his daughter that I felt altogether powerless to alleviate.

Sometimes, now, I began to have trouble sleeping, and would lie awake for hours thinking and listening to the breathing of my husband as he lay next to me. Every so often, the steady rhythm of inhale and exhale would suddenly be interrupted by a long, deep sigh, almost like a woeful moan. Those troubled sighs tinged the darkness around me with a deep uneasiness, and cast stones upon what had but so recently become the placid waters of my nights. Could some flaw, some crack, a tiny chink, perhaps, have developed in the perfect, seamless façade of my made-for-TV family? With resolute determination, I attempted to push such thoughts from my consciousness.

While Lora was growing more distant and detached from us, her brother, Mike, continued his regular weekend visits, rarely betraying even a suspicion of the deep pain and resentment his parents' divorce had inflicted upon him. Bruce became very attached to his half brother. They would play cars and "hotwheels" together by the hour and, when it was time for Mike to go back to his mother's home, Bruce would often cling to his legs and beg him to stay. It would still be several years before I learned that the much older Mike, in sudden fits of rage, would sometimes take out his resentments upon my son, hurling him against the wall as the two "played" alone together in the bedroom. Mike was very envious because Bruce had his dad full time, while he could only be with Butch on weekends. Mike's emotional scars would be a long time healing.

*

*   *

As much as Bruce loved playing cars with Mike, he also enjoyed playing dolls with Tanya. In fact, he probably enjoyed playing dolls even more than his sister did, while Tanya could be quite the tomboy at times. Butch and I weren't terribly concerned about our son's attachment to girlish trappings. Gender role playing, much of which, I am convinced, is learned, can fluxuate in young children and we did not wish to shame Bruce into repressing the softer side of his nature in favor of some overly exaggerated masculinity. We simply considered it a childhood phase and something that could even be beneficial to our son in the future, developing his nurturing side and making him a better father someday. Still, his fondness for things feminine caused some eyebrows to rise, and inspired numerous snide remarks about Bruce's "peculiarity" from some of the more cerebrally challenged among my husband's family. Interestingly enough, no one ever looked askance at our daughter's fondness for climbing trees and playing baseball.

One summer afternoon I was taking sun in the yard and watching my three-year-old boy play. He called out to me that he was going into the house and would be right back. He was gone for several minutes, but just at the point when I was about to go to see what he was up to, he emerged from the back door. To my astonishment, Bruce had draped himself in some articles of my clothing. He spoke with an older, feminine air and introduced himself as "Marcy." Then Marcy began to tell me her story: She had lived before and had been killed in an automobile accident. She talked about another place, another life, another family. I was stunned into complete silence, and did my best not to overreact to my son's performance.

Presently, Marcy went back into the house and a few minutes later Bruce returned to the yard.

Now, I did not believe in reincarnation, but obviously Bruce's acting out of this highly developed female persona was very strongly motivated. Marcy appeared several more times, and my husband even witnessed some of these episodes. He was as totally flabbergasted as I. We both agreed, however, that it was better not to make a big deal out of what, in our estimation, had to be nothing more than some kind of child's game. After all, children's rapidly developing imagination often inspires them to create made-up friends and playmates. Following one such occurrence, however, Butch and I speculated openly to each other that Bruce might indeed be gay. But we quickly dismissed this notion as ridiculous, especially considering our son's tender age. As suddenly as the Marcy episodes had begun, they ceased. When I asked Bruce about them several years later, he insisted he had no idea what I was talking about.

As a child, Bruce was quite the charmer. (He still is, for that matter). Women were especially fond of him. My friend, Nancy Siefker, always said, "He's a special child. Bruce is destined to do something big, someday."

Nancy's attachment to Bruce began even before he was born. I met her in a bowling league. Though it was somewhat out of character for me, because of my intense shyness, I was putting forth an extra effort to make new friends in an attempt to get over the trauma of my two miscarriages. I had added my name to a list of "fillers" looking for teams in need of new members. As a result, I was assigned to Nancy's team. She is such a warm and outgoing person, it is difficult not to like her instantly, and we quickly became very close friends. When I became pregnant with Bruce, wanting to take every precaution, I decided I had to give up bowling. But Nancy kept in close contact, and was always there to bolster my flagging spirits whenever I became depressed and frightened. If she could not drop by to see me, she would usually call to find out how I was getting along. One particularly gloomy winter's day she sent me a beautiful spring bouquet with a card that read, "Hang in there! Spring is just around the corner," knowing that Bruce's due date was in April. Nancy always joked that Bruce was her most difficult pregnancy.

When my son started kindergarten he instantly became popular with his teachers and classmates. I invited the entire class to his birthday party. Both of my children had many friends as soon as they started school. Our house became the epicenter of neighborhood juvenile activity. We played host to an endless stream of slumber parties, wiener roasts, birthday celebrations, backyard camp-outs and Halloween and Christmas parties. I was June Cleaver gone into overdrive. For me, it had been the end of my sixth-grade year before I made my first real friend at school. Even then, my schoolmates rarely visited our house. It was easy to see that things were definitely turning out much better for my kids than they had been for me.

One day, when Tanya was about eight years old, while I was giving her a bath, she looked up at me with her big, dark eyes and, in a heart-piercing little voice she said, "Mommy, am I adopted?" I was completely astounded at this question. "Tanya, baby," I soothed, trying not to betray any trace of my sudden consternation, "you've always known that you are adopted." She appeared devastated by this. I was bewildered and more than a little unsettled.

On the early advice of her case worker, I had always been open with Tanya about her adoption. I bought her storybooks about children who were adopted and from the moment she had started to ask questions I had been scrupulously honest, believing this the best policy in the long run. In fact, I had made a very serious mistake. For, as things turned out, it was only now, at age eight, that my daughter had actually begun to have a clear understanding of what adoption is, and what it meant to her to be an adopted child. It had simply been too abstract a concept for her to fully grasp when she was younger. That day, as she sat there among the soap bubbles, I witnessed an abstruse and implacable sadness being born in my daughter's eyes, a sadness that would remain there for many years yet to come. This sadness arose out of a profound sense of abandonment, which nothing I could ever say seemed to have any power to assuage. Soon her feelings of abandonment would deepen into bitterness and a smoldering rage that would sometimes flare into overt anger and hostility.

The adoption of Tanya had brought me only joy and happiness. I did not even want to consider that being adopted could have caused her pain in any way. The contemplation of that was much too complex and frightening for me, so, true to my form at the time, I pushed it right out of my mind. Though I wanted to simply forget my daughter was adopted, from then on Tanya never could.

So, I would simply have to try harder, plan more outings, bake more cookies, have more birthday parties, become more involved at church. All the while, deep within myself, I was harboring two secret fears that gnawed at my insides like rats at a cracker barrel. They were of the type of fear that one dare not speak aloud. For if you let them escape the confines of your body, past the threshold of your lips, they could all too easily become terrible realities. And that, you are certain, would be more than you could bear. It would surely mean your complete undoing. One of those dark fears was that my daughter would reject me as her mother. The other was that my beloved son would turn out to be gay.

CHAPTER IV

By the time Bruce entered third grade, I began to notice that the number of boys among his playmates had dwindled significantly. Now, he seemed to play almost altogether with the little girls in our neighborhood. Bruce was confused by the other boys' apparent rejection of him and so was I.

One day, while walking home from school, a group of sixth grade boys attacked him. While one of these bigger boys held him, the others took turns punching Bruce in the stomach. As I found out much later, he was grateful the boys had not hit him in the face, thereby not leaving any outward telltale injuries. He was so ashamed of having been beaten up, and the lack of visible injuries meant he wouldn't have to explain to his parents. It was as though Bruce seemed to feel he deserved it. So, in a way very similar to the suffering my mother had endured twenty years earlier because of her disfigurement, my son was now beginning to internalize feelings of guilt simply because he was different from the other children.

School was gradually becoming a nightmare for him. I could see the dread and stress building up as the end of his summer vacations would approach and the time to return to school drew nearer.

My husband was working hard to find common ground with Bruce. With each passing year, it just seemed they shared fewer and fewer interests. When Butch discovered that his son was fascinated with go-carts, he immediately went out and bought one. Though we could hardly afford the additional expense, the two of them would spend many hours together working on that little car, and it provided a kind of bridge between father and son. So, as it turned out, the go-cart was a very wise investment.

When Bruce joined the Cub Scouts, Butch also joined the Cub Scouts, becoming the assistant scout master. This gave my husband an opportunity to observe Bruce in his interactions with the other boys. Butch began to notice that our son did not appear to enjoy many of the activities that boys his age were supposed to take to "naturally." He would hang back from group activities, was losing interest and often did not feel much like going to Cub Scout meetings. Then another little boy, by the name of Scott, joined the troop. He exhibited many of the same interests, behavioral patterns and mannerism as did our son. After Scott became a Cub Scout, Bruce began to show a good deal more interest in participating. Though we did not know for certain then that Bruce was gay (at least that's what we kept telling ourselves), we knew he was different and it was obvious that he and Scott were different in very much the same way. Bruce worked hard at scouting and earned the Arrow of Light, the highest honor for a Webelos Cub Scout.

His fifth-grade teacher was a man. Bruce always got on well with his female teachers, but from the men he sometimes received ridicule and harassment. Even though it was, and still is (at least as of this writing) against federal law to do so, this particular teacher would often read directly from the Bible to his class of fifth graders. Apparently he was very devout, and would sometimes employ religiously based admonishments concerning the children's behavior. When Halloween rolled around, this teacher asked his students to raise their hands if they were planning on going out trick-or-treating. He then proceeded to inform them that dressing up like ghosts and goblins and going trick-or-treating on Halloween night was doing the work of Satan. And he wasn't joking, either. The man made it very clear that he was absolutely serious. After learning of this episode from Bruce, feeling it was not a teacher's place to force his religious views upon my child, I went to the principal of the school and objected. Out of concern for the possible repercussions for my son, however, I asked the principal not to reveal my identity to the teacher. The very next day, when Bruce arrived at school, the teacher proceeded to publicly humiliate him before his entire class for having complained to the principal. This, among other things, of course only added to Bruce's growing alienation and ostracism at school. The Halloween incident, and a few others still to come, eventually convinced me that most administrators and several teachers in the school system simply could not be trusted where my son was concerned.

Teasing and other harassment from his fellow students escalated throughout school from then on. The recess at lunchtime was one of the worst periods of the day for Bruce. The abuse during this "break" was relentless and intolerable. I took to picking him up for lunch in order to allow him at least an hour of peace during the school day. Returning Bruce each afternoon became one of the most difficult things I had to do. I watched him climb out of the car, looking as if he was carrying the weight of the world upon his little boy's shoulders, and it was simply heart-wrenching for me. There seemed so little I could do about his plight. Then he would square those heavily laden young shoulders, take a deep breath and give me a last, fleeting glance before pushing open the door to the building and walking reluctantly inside. It was as though he was entering some hazardous environment from which I was barred, where I had no control. I felt as if I were abandoning him to a most hostile fate.

In the afternoon, when he returned home from school, Bruce would head from the front door straight to the television set to watch his favorite program, a game show for children hosted by a good-looking, male teenager. As soon as the broadcast had concluded, Bruce would switch to a channel from another city so as to watch the same show all over again from beginning to end. It was difficult to ignore how fascinated he was with this particular program. One evening, while checking Bruce's homework assignments in his notebook, I came across a story he had written. It was a love story about the youthful game show host and a girl. The story was written in the first person from the girl's perspective and her voice was clearly the voice of my son. I was shocked beyond all belief. My hands trembled as I turned the pages of this story, and I struggled to fight back tears. For here I was, face to face with the first real piece of tangible, incontrovertible evidence that my ten-year-old boy was gay. I didn't want to believe it. In fact, I refused to believe it. But, though I would continue in some form of denial for quite a while yet, in retrospect it is clear to me that from that day on I knew in my heart our son was gay.

I sought the help of a counselor in order to find a way to assist Bruce in dealing with the unrelenting onslaught of verbal and physical harassment he was enduring at school. The first session with this man I attended alone, and I used it as an opportunity to confide in him my suspicions concerning my son's homosexuality. The counselor asked me who was the very first person Bruce had ever had a strong infatuation with. It was my friend, Nancy. At age four, as little boys often do with older women, Bruce had even proposed marriage to her. With this information in mind, the counselor referred to some grand, psychological study (the title of which now escapes me completely), and reassured me that my boy was not likely to be gay. I would cling tenaciously to this shred of "evidence" like Linus to his tattered security blanket for several years to come.

*

* *

At about this same time my teen-aged daughter's anger and frustration, which had been simmering below the surface for several years, exploded into hate-filled eruptions of maniacal rage and aggressive belligerence, which, more often than not, she directed at my husband and me. This situation reached a critical stage after her break-up with a certain boyfriend. Butch and I decided it was time to find professional help.

We sat with her therapist through many painful, angry sessions, during which Tanya never for a moment stopped glaring at us with her bitter, hostile eyes, impervious to all our attempts to help and understand her. "They have been nothing but good to me," she said on one occasion, referring to Butch and me. "I know that they love me. But I don't want their love!"

Through a numbing, pain-induced fog, I heard the doctor explaining to my husband and me that what Tanya was expressing was misplaced anger at having been abandoned by her birth mother. The emotionally devastating break-up with the boyfriend, perceived by Tanya as yet another abandonment, was the crucial element that had led directly to this crisis. It was as if she felt we were going to abandon her as well, and wanted to give us sufficient reason to do so, thereby avoiding yet another devastating rejection. She would reject us first, before we had the chance to do what all the others seemed to have done.

Finally, we all agreed, including Tanya herself, that she needed to spend some time in a private psychiatric hospital. She was admitted to Our Lady of Peace, a mental health facility located in Louisville, Kentucky, over fifty miles away from us. She was there for nearly a month. After her release the long process of building a new relationship with her began. At first, it was like living with a stranger. All we could do was give her space and wait.

There were fewer and fewer delusions left for me to hide behind, concerning the rubble that remained of my tidy little "50s sit-com" family. Those fantasies had all vanished like a puff of smoke in a tornado the night I left my daughter in a lonely ward of that psychiatric hospital many miles from our home. I had failed with what had mattered most in my life: my children. They were hurting, seriously hurting, and I was seemingly incapable of doing anything to make things right. I had no more answers. All those pat, naive, little TV-script solutions of mine had finally been exhausted. Now, there were only questions, haunting, unrelenting and dismayingly insoluble questions.

Whether I was ready to admit it to myself or not, I had reached the point where I didn't know what I believed in anymore, or indeed if I believed in anything at all. Life had ceased to make much sense to me. It felt as if I had been sold a bill of goods. I had played strictly by the rules. I had not simply become more involved in our church, I had served it in every possible capacity of which I was capable. I did not simply care for my family, I was devoted to it. This was not the way things were supposed to turn out. You're supposed to reap what you sow, right? I was sure I had not sown this bitter harvest.

The long descent into the dark night of my soul had begun in earnest, but this was only a prelude to the struggles, despair and the wrenching spiritual and emotional crisis that was waiting just ahead for me and my family.

CHAPTER

V

The woman who had left me the little ceramic figure of the praying hands, back during the time when I was in the hospital fighting the near-miscarriage of my son, had planted a seed in my soul. That seed had fallen upon fertile ground and had begun to grow to form the basis for my faith and a highly personal apprehension of spiritual beliefs. The idea of a God who actually suffered with us was a startlingly revolutionary notion for me. I held this concept up before my mind's eye and examined it like a many-faceted, precious gemstone. The God of my childhood was a cold, distant, severe deity, set high on his throne of judgement. The image of a God who felt our pain and suffered with us was completely foreign to my strictly fundamentalist upbringing. This view created a kind of restlessness in me, a hunger, a need to search for deeper spiritual truths than any that had occurred or had been presented to me before. I found myself reading the Bible as much to pick it apart as to find spiritual reassurance and comfort. I felt I could no longer accept the Bible unquestioningly simply as the unerring, revealed truth of God, the way I had been taught to do from childhood. Still, the more I read it, the more I believed it truly to be inspired by God. A friend, with whom I had shared my desire for greater spiritual understanding, encouraged me to start attending that tiny country church I alluded to earlier in my story.

The Oak Grove Presbyterian Church was actually more like a kind of family chapel, it was so small. When I came to it, it was a dying rural church, with only about twelve or fifteen regularly attending members left in its congregation. What attracted me, however, was the woman pastor. She spoke of the empathetic God I was seeking, and her words rang true in my heart and in my mind. She encouraged me to study and to question the scriptures, and provided just the inspiration I needed to take my first tentative steps into a new dimension of faith. As I mentioned earlier, Oak Grove was the church where my husband and infant son had been baptized together. Unfortunately, it was but a short time after we joined the little congregation that its dynamic woman pastor, who had so quickly become my mentor, left the church.

It appeared impossible for such an insignificant, and admittedly unattractive, parish to lure a new, full-time pastor. The building was small and in need of much repair. The congregation had dwindled away and those of us who were left could hardly be considered affluent. The days when bright young men and women of God would have considered a situation such as ours a welcome challenge to their calling had long since vanished with the winds of self-possessed avarice that still sweep depredatingly across our country, poisoning with greed everything in their path. Finally, one of the members brought in a schoolbus driver who was also a lay preacher in the Baptist church. One sermon, I recall in particular, was entitled: "Imagine Being a Kitchen Match in Hell for Eternity," or "Who Are You Taking to Hell with You?" I was back to square one. This was like returning to the Pentecostal faith of my childhood. It was very discouraging.

Our rescue from the fires of hell came, in this particular case at least, in the form of a bone-freezing blizzard. A raging snow storm provided us with the unlikely impetus for looking into attending another church. The snow had left the rural roads impassible, so we decided to attend the Grace Presbyterian Church in Sunnyside, rather than chancing the drive, or just staying home.

The sermon that Sunday was most impressive, and the minister's lucid and well thought-out exegesis of his Biblical text contrasted dramatically with the simple, literal interpretation of scripture so characteristic of the unsophisticated religious teaching of my youth.

The congregation of Grace Presbyterian was of a different social stratum than we were. It was made up almost altogether of doctors, dentists, lawyers, teachers and business types — the professional elite of the town. For many of them, our presence at church represented the first time they had encountered the "working class" in any kind of a "social" setting. Though curious about us, the people seemed extremely friendly and welcoming when we approached them to introduce ourselves. My husband and I concluded almost immediately that, despite the class disparity, this was a church where we could come to feel comfortable socially and grow spiritually and intellectually. It was tempting to view that blizzard truly as an act of divine providence.

We attended with extreme regularity, the same way I had done as a small child. Even while on summer camping trips at Lake Monroe, some forty miles away, we would drive back to Sunnyside on Sunday mornings, returning to our campsite following services. We were eager to serve the church in any capacity. We worked as deacons, elders, Sunday-school teachers, lay worship leaders, choir members and on every imaginable committee. With any project, such as decorating the sanctuary for Advent, for example, we were always the first to arrive and the last to depart. It was important to serve the needs of our church, but we were also determined to please our new friends as well. They were rapidly becoming like family to us, and we readily took to our roles as caregivers and obligers. Like Arthur Miller's Willy Loman, it was so important to us to be "well liked," and we were sure that we were just that.

Many in our new church were attracted by my inquisitive faith, and were also amazed by my personal interpretations of scripture. I think my humble origins and simple, straightforward approach contributed to the general astonishment. They had never considered a person like me to be capable of doing much creative thinking on her own. Most of them had been born into the church, and it had never occurred to them to interrogate their beliefs. They had simply accepted blindly the faith that had been handed down to them by their parents. I came to be widely admired among my church family, and I eagerly lapped it up. I needed their admiration, even at the risk of taking upon myself a heavy burden of dysfunctional codependancy.

It was my first real exposure to educated people, and whole new worlds were beginning to open up before me. Suddenly I was being invited into the elegant and expensive homes of physicians, merchants and lawyers, and having my ideas and opinions listened to and, seemingly, respected. I also took note as these people voiced their deep, often even prayerful, concerns over the diminishing returns they were receiving on their numerous investments, while my family was living from one paycheck to the next. I heard them agonizing over having their fine homes professionally redecorated, while my husband and I were hard at work re-roofing our modest bungalow with our own, bare hands. A three-cent-per-gallon increase in the price of gasoline, or an unexpectedly high light bill could call for significant budgetary adjustments in the Murray household, but very little set those well-heeled residential establishments reeling, complain though their inhabitants might about the outrageous price of such basic necessities as new draperies for the bay window. I was witnessing an exotic, extraordinary side of life that before I had considered probably only existed (if in fact it existed at all) in places like New York, Chicago and L.A., or perhaps only in the movies, not in little old Sunnyside, Indiana. And here I found myself miraculously at the center of this strange, new world. It was pretty heady stuff for a small-town girl, and from the wrong side of the tracks at that.

But it also gradually became abundantly clear to me that the day to day struggles my husband and I endured had made us stronger. We did not devote much of our energy to whining about this, that or the other of life's trials and tribulations. There simply was no time nor need for such idle self-indulgence. We were too busy making ends meet and trying to enjoy as intensely as possible the time that was otherwise left to us.

As I delved deeper into scripture, I became increasingly troubled by my study of the Old Testament. There was so much here that I simply couldn't seem to reconcile my heart to. Passages that stated God's displeasure with the Israelites because they refused to slay the children of conquered peoples I found particularly upsetting. If I could accept into my heart a God who demanded the slaughter of innocent children, then what kind of a person would that make me? If this were to become my image of God, would I not be bound to pattern myself after that image, at least to some degree? I once approached a minister about my struggle. I asked him why he thought the God of the Old Testament was so different from the God of the New Testament. Had God changed, or did man's perception of him change? The very idea of scripture being influenced by human perceptions unsettled this pastor to such an extent that he brusquely, and really quite amazingly, responded that God had in fact changed!

One story from the Old Testament that disturbed me profoundly, and still haunts me somewhat to this very day, was the tale of Abraham and his near sacrificial slaughter of his beloved son, Isaac, at the request of God himself. According to the story, God demanded that Abraham demonstrate his total obedience by journeying with his son into the land of Moriah and there offer up Isaac as a burnt sacrifice. Only at the last moment, when Abraham is about to plunge a dagger into the heart of his dear son, does God send an angel to stay his hand.

I read this story over and over. We discussed it at length in my Bible study class, and I consulted the writings of various esteemed theologians, whose books I had discovered in the library of Grace Presbyterian shortly after joining the church. But these learned biblical scholars rarely agreed upon the tale of Abraham and Isaac. In an attempt to make the story appear more palatable, they often seemed to jump from point "A" to point "C" without ever dealing with what came in between. Some would say that God was jealous, and wanted to test Abraham's faith, while others would state that God was already aware of Abraham's faith, but wanted to reveal its depth to Abraham himself. Still other theologians insisted that Abraham knew God would not make him carry out this murderous demand because of the covenant between God and Abraham, which said that Abraham would be the founder of a great nation.

But no one ever considered young Isaac! It seemed clear to me that Isaac was not a willing participant in this little ruse of God's. Otherwise, why did he have to be bound? I imagined the boy's confusion and terror. How could a father be so eagerly oblivious to his own son's life? How could a loving God make such a dreadful request in the first place? Why did Abraham not consider sacrificing himself instead of his beloved child? Would this act not have been just as great a testimony of love? The questions were endless, and would give me no peace.

One day, when Bruce was but a toddler, he was awkwardly trying to take his first steps on his own. After several repeated attempts, he managed two or three before he started to tumble. My hands reached out to catch him and steady him on his tiny feet. Suddenly I was caught up in a moment of spiritual insight. As my son's small hand reached out trustingly to my much larger one, time suddenly stood still and my own hand became as the hand of God while my child's small hand was as my own. In an instant everything became clear as crystal to me: God relates to us as any loving parent would. He rejoices over our clumsy first steps, and He lifts us up when we fall. His expectations of us are attuned with our capabilities. I would never be angry with my toddler because he could not run as swiftly as I could. No loving parent, not in need of psychological analysis and therapy, would ever set up cruel tests to make her child prove his love or loyalty. Likewise, I suddenly knew with complete certainty that God's compassion for his children could not possibly be any less than mine for my own child. Everything else was simply mythology, the human invention of a multitude of authors, retellers and scribes over the centuries for their own, now obscure, reasons. Of this I could not now be more convinced. Tears of joy, and relief, streamed down my cheeks as I scooped Bruce up into my arms and danced with him merrily about the room, much to his great delight. My child had been for me the messenger of God.

CHAPTER VI

My faith in God and commitment to the church intensified. I seemed unable to get enough of participating in parish activities. I joined the bell choir and, a little later on, the adult choir that sang at all Sunday services. Choir rehearsal was on Wednesday evenings. It quickly became my favorite night of the week. I took tremendous pleasure in learning about the rich musical heritage of the church, from Afro-American spirituals to Bach cantatas. I also enjoyed the wonderful sense of fellowship and camaraderie that only a musical ensemble can inspire in its members. A great singer I was not, but I delighted in the effort.

My daughter did not share the keen interest in church life of the rest of her family. Tanya viewed Grace Presbyterian with an intense wariness that bordered on outright contempt. She was appalled by what she considered to be my naive refusal to recognize the blatant hypocrisy of my fellow church-goers. At the time this reaction appeared to me to be simply another manifestation of the mounting rebellion, seemingly against nearly everything, that characterized so much of Tanya's teen-age years. I simply refused to recognize that there might be a kernel of wisdom in her derisive caveats.

From as early as age eight, Bruce had begun to want to take part in the sacrament of Holy Communion. One of my many duties was the preparation of the elements of bread and wine (or grape juice, as that is what some of my fellow Presbyterians preferred) the night before the service.

Many times Bruce would help me. He always exhibited such reverence on these occasions that Butch and I decided the time had come to enroll him in classes in preparation for his first Communion. It was at a Maundy Thursday service that Bruce was first allowed at the Lord's table. Butch and I presented him with a gold cross in honor of the occasion.

Our son was following in his parents' footsteps. He seemed almost to gravitate toward the church. Often when an acolyte would fail to show up to light the candles on Communion Sundays, Bruce would eagerly fill in. He would seek out elderly women, quite often ignored and forgotten, who always sat in the very last pews, to give them a welcoming hug. Everyone commented on what a good boy he was and a benefit to our congregation. Bruce loved the church deeply in return. If anything, his enthusiasm exceeded even that of his parents.

The pastor at this time, Rev. Saunders, was a frequent visitor in our home. One afternoon, during one of his impromptu calls, he noticed Bruce lying on his stomach on the floor with pencils and paper. Pastor Saunders inquired as to what he might be drawing. Bruce excitedly explained that it was a fashion design, and went on to narrate, in enthusiastic detail, his desire to become a designer of women's clothes when he grew up.

The expression of concerned dismay that crossed the pastor's face was unmistakable. Later, in horrified whispers, Rev. Saunders inquired if I had ever considered that Bruce might be gay. A chill ran through my body. It felt as though someone had just walked on my grave. I denied my fears to him, but I wanted to know what Rev. Saunders thought about homosexuality. As it turned out, he did not think it was a choice, but equated it to a craving kind of disease such as drug addiction or alcoholism. So, before my son had even entered adolescence, I heard him compared to alcoholics and junkies for the very first time. Sadly, it would not be the last.

As Bruce started middle school, the girls who had become such good friends with him in the lower grades began to pull away. They wanted to date, and when they found out that he had not the least romantic inclination toward them they simply lost interest in maintaining a relationship with him. Fortunately, he still had his friend Scott, who had confided to Bruce that he was gay. Bruce talked with me about this on occasion. He said he wasn't going to "hold it against" Scott. They hung out with a couple of other boys, and Bruce would sometimes mention this or that "foxy girl" they had seen. Butch and I eagerly seized upon these fragments of "proof" that our son was going to turn out to be straight after all, so desperate were we to avoid admitting to ourselves what was becoming increasingly unavoidable. Looking back, I can understand that in many ways Bruce was actually trying to protect us by behaving as he sensed society expected him to. We had, in subtle ways (and some probably not so subtle) undoubtedly communicated our anxieties to him, and he was reacting out of his own internalized homophobia.

Pop diva Janet Jackson became Bruce's idol. (Stupidly, I fooled myself into believing he had a crush on her). His room was plastered with her posters, and he started dressing in black as she did. Of course the other students in seventh grade immediately perceived him as different or "weird." But to them "weird," in this particular instance, meant "satanic" because of his insistence upon dressing entirely in black. Oddly enough, our purchase of a black car about this time also served to fuel these rumors. One teacher even went so far as to report to the principal that Bruce was strongly suspected of being involved in occult practices. My son, as devout a follower of Jesus Christ as any boy his age anywhere, found himself called into the principal's office to answer to charges of devil worship simply because he wore black clothes and his parents drove a black sedan. Could burning at the stake be far behind, I wondered?

By eighth grade, however, the label had gradually mutated from satanic to homo and faggot which, in reality, turned out to be far worse than getting yourself accused of being the prince of darkness incarnate. Interestingly, two of Bruce's former friends, who became his most vociferous tormentors during this period, were in fact gay themselves, as we learned a very few short years later.

In despair, Bruce sought the counsel of a woman teacher whom he admired and who he trusted would be compassionate. To his astonishment, she told him flatly that all the abuse and rejection he was suffering was entirely his own fault. "You ought to try harder to fit in," she sternly advised him. "Mainstream yourself. You're too different. You should change."

One male teacher did recognize Bruce's predicament. He tried to be encouraging by telling him to just hang in there until he got to high school. In high school everything would be different, this teacher said, because the students there were more mature.

At home I felt increasingly helpless as I watched our son's spirit slowly dying before my very eyes. The phone never rang for Bruce. No friends came to call. Even at church, I had noticed, people had begun to distance themselves from him. I knew his days at school were miserable and filled with torment, and the sad desperation of his evenings and weekends was palpable. I was deeply afraid for him, as much for what he might do to himself as for what some school-yard punk might do to him.

At last I decided that I had to find out the truth, whatever the cost. My husband and I would deal with it as best we could. To hell with protecting my own precious comfort level, which I had come increasingly to realize was exactly what I'd been doing all this time. My son's life was what mattered here. If he was gay, I had to know it. How else could we begin to help him? The bomb that had been hanging over my family for so long now was going to have to fall. It had become clear that we stood a good chance of losing Bruce otherwise.

Recently I had run across an article in an Indianapolis newspaper about an organization for teenage gays called IYG (Indiana Youth Group). I had clipped this piece from the paper and saved it until I thought the time was appropriate. With all the nonchalance I was capable of, under the circumstances, I handed it to Bruce one morning. "Did you know they actually have a support group for gay teens?" I said, smiling brightly. "I think it's a great idea! If you know anyone at school who can benefit from this information, why don't you pass it along to them?"

I should have been given the Academy Award for my performance that day. I searched his eyes, as I handed over the strip of newsprint. A flash of something that looked like hope seemed to cross Bruce's face, a look I hadn't seen there in months. Then, just as suddenly, his expression dissolved into one of unmistakable fear. "O.K., mom," he said meekly, his eyes cast downward as he turned to go.

For the next few days I watched Bruce carefully. Had I done the wrong thing? Was I too pushy? Perhaps I should have waited. My anxiety was driving me crazy, almost to the point of physical illness. I could tell he was distressed. He was quiet and more withdrawn than usual, and he spent even more time alone in his room. One evening I noticed he was taking a very long time in the shower. *What was he doing in there?* I fretted.

As it turned out, all the time he was showering Bruce had been composing a letter in his mind that he planned to write and leave for me to read when he went out. In the letter he would tell me that he was gay. That his life had been hanging by a thread as he tried to make up his mind which would cause his parents the least pain — their son's suicide or discovering he was "queer." Seeing how people's mere speculations he might be gay had caused him to be so thoroughly despised and rejected by society, he had been leaning heavily toward committing suicide. After all, wouldn't a quick death be better than a lifetime of painful ridicule and ostracism for him and humiliation for his family? But the article I had given him stayed his hand. It had made him think that perhaps there was some alternative, a chance, a way out of the nightmare. Maybe he wasn't so completely alone after all.

It was a letter he would never need to write. He passed the chair where I was sitting, as he crossed the room on his way to get a note pad and pencil. On impulse I took his hand in mine, gently halting his progression. "Bruce, honey," I said, looking up into those eyes, so sad and frightened I could hardly bare to hold their gaze. "Are you gay?"

If I live to be two hundred I will never forget the look of pure agony that contorted my son's face in that long, silent moment of terror. "Yes!" he blurted out at last. "Yes, yes, yes!" And he collapsed, sobbing uncontrollably into my lap.

I felt surely my heart would break, so painful was it for me to witness my child's terrible suffering. "It's all right, baby," I murmured, stroking his hair. "Mommy is here." I fought back my own tears as I lifted up his face and covered it with my kisses. "I love you, always have, always will. You won't have to deal with this alone anymore. We'll handle it as a family from now on. We're in this together," I declared, masking my many grave misgivings behind a façade of sympathy and reassurance.

Gradually, I could hear the agony in his voice change to relief as he told me how he had planned to come out to me that evening, after I'd read his letter. He explained that, though still terrified at the prospect of telling me, he was willing to risk it because of the newspaper clipping I'd given him, and because of the promise that little article had held of his being able to meet other young people who were like him. (I still thank God for providing me the courage to overcome my fears and give Bruce that article.) I assured him we would get in contact with support groups for young gays, that we would do whatever it took.

"But, please," he whispered. "We mustn't tell dad."

I was deeply shocked. "Son, you know your father will stand behind you," I said. "Your dad loves you very much."

"Do you think he'd understand?" Bruce said, sounding very unconvinced.

I declared my absolute belief Butch would indeed understand, though I was far from convinced that "understand" was a word I could yet apply even to myself. I was trying to be supportive, but decades of enforced ignorance and conditioned prejudice would still have to be overcome before any real understanding of what it means to be gay would dawn in me. At that moment all I had to sustain me was my deep love for my child. I clung to that love desperately, as one who is drowning clings to a life preserver. For love was what would have to carry me across a virtual sea of benighted fear that stretched between me and the kind of real empathy that would make acceptance of Bruce's homosexuality possible.

That night I lay awake for a very long time after my husband had drifted off to sleep. Should I wake him and turn his world upside down just as mine had been earlier that day? Should I allow him one last night of peaceful sleep? I could hear the bomb screaming as it neared its mark. I felt the impact and violent explosion deep in my already tortured soul. My life was shattered. Only two short weeks before my unmarried daughter, now eighteen years of age, had announced she was pregnant. I felt the darkness pressing in on me, threatening to suffocate me. Closer and closer it hovered like some great, ominous bird with engulfing, black wings. I felt myself slipping toward panic. At last, unable to withstand the pressure alone, I turned to my husband, as I had done so many times before. Gently waking Butch, I recounted to him the events of the day. After a moment's silence, he sighed deeply and said: "My only fear is for how the world will treat our son. — He is a good boy, though. He's such a good boy." For many hours, Butch lay there silently holding me in his arms, fending off the darkness until at last I fell asleep sometime just before dawn.

The next day, after Bruce had departed for school, I cried almost nonstop. I couldn't seem to help myself. It was impossible for me to function in any kind of normal, routine way. Ugly whispers from the past returned to torment me. Vile, hideous memories came into sharp focus in my mind. I remembered how the town had gone crazy with rumors and gossip several years back when a childhood friend of mine had been brutally murdered. But the whisperers were far more concerned with the fact that the murder had occurred outside an Indianapolis gay bar than with the crushing tragedy of Steve's death itself. The stories that circulated about him were like sick, obscene jokes told by people who sometimes snickered behind their hands afterward. I recalled the two women on the bowling league who everyone thought were lesbians. I remembered the nasty things the other women said about them and how they were almost universally shunned. They seemed so grateful even for the smile I sometimes gave them, but I was far too afraid of the reaction of the rest of the group to speak openly to them. I thought of the boy, in my brother's rock band, who had come out. He was very talented both as a musician and as an artist, and had lovingly given my mother many works of art that still adorned the walls of her home. He was devoted to my brother and his band. But when he moved away to Texas to be with his lover and eventually died of AIDS, this wonderful, gentle, gifted young man suddenly became something less than human in the minds of the local people who had known him. He too became the brunt of those sick, obscene jokes, almost the same jokes that had gone around about Steve. And I remembered a so-called "research paper" that had been circulated by a doctor at our community hospital. It depicted in graphic detail several bizarre and disgusting sexual practices, involving bestiality, human excrement and urine, that the author claimed to have "statistical proof" were common among gay men. The thought of my handsome, loving son involved in such vile, filthy and degrading activities was more than I could bear. Like most of my fellow Americans, these were the kinds of mental images of gay people that my society had presented me with and had continually reinforced for as far back as I could remember.

Before Bruce returned home from school in the afternoon, I washed my face with cool water to reduce the swelling around my eyes. I didn't want him to know I had been crying. I brushed my hair and then went to the kitchen to start cooking supper, trying to make everything seem as normal as possible.

Butch had picked our son up at school that evening. "How was the ride home?" I inquired of Bruce, as he passed through the kitchen. "Just fine," he replied. "Thanks, mom, for not telling him."

"So, then he acted the same as always?" I asked.

"Well, yeah, sure." Bruce looked a little puzzled.

"He knows," I said.

At that moment, Butch entered the kitchen. "Yes, son, I know," he said. "And I want you to understand that I love you and there is nothing will ever change that."

As I watched them hug each other warmly, I thanked God I would not be put through the agony of being forced to choose between my husband and my son. That at least had been spared me. But there were still hundreds of other questions and doubts warring and raging inside my brain. Just knowing the truth had not suddenly made everything seem exactly rosy. If anything, it had simply opened up Pandora's box. I was deeply afraid.

*

*   *

Looking back on the first several weeks following Bruce's coming out to us, I really don't know how I managed to put one foot in front of the other, let alone be supportive and do what needed to be done for my son. I was getting almost no sleep nights, and my days were filled with tears and worry. I found out the address of the nearest chapter of IYG. It met in a feminist bookstore located in the university town of Bloomington, Indiana, some fifty miles to the northwest of Sunnyside. My husband and I drove Bruce to his first meeting. I felt like I might be sick to my stomach, as I watched him walk through the door, though another part of me was also pleased and happy that we were taking a positive step.

Inside myself I was being torn apart. I had started doing a lot of reading to find out everything I could about homosexuality and gay issues. My mind, therefore, kept telling me that we were doing the right thing, that the youth group was the best first step, and we were on the road to sorting this thing out. My emotions, on the other hand, kept screaming something else, that this whole business was abhorrent, immoral, probably sinful, definitely something to be ashamed of and to keep hidden. Obviously, at that point in my life, the very idea of anyone back in Sunnyside discovering the truth filled me with absolute terror. I felt I could tell no one, not my best friend, not even my mother. I remembered our minister once saying that in conflicts between mind and gut, the gut would win out every time. I hoped and prayed he was wrong, because if my gut reaction triumphed over my mind then it was going to be my son who ended up the loser. Fortunately, my heart, which was still filled to overflowing with love for Bruce, was strongly allied with my mind in this particular case.

Butch and I waited two hours outside in the parking lot while Bruce attended that first IYG meeting. I kept looking at my watch, and when the time reached five minutes past the hour when the meeting was to have ended, I began strongly urging my husband to go into that building and bring our son out, by force if necessary. Fortunately, before I could talk Butch into what would have been a really very destructively stupid move, the door of the bookstore opened and I saw Bruce walking toward the car. He was grinning from ear to ear.

"It was great, mom," he said. "Now I know I have a chance at some kind of a happy life. I never could even have imagined that before."

I was elated. We *did* make the right decision, I thought. For a moment a glimmer of hope that things might just work out broke through to me. That glimmer, however, was short lived. I noticed a boy standing behind my son. "Mom, dad," Bruce said, presenting his new friend. "This is Jason."

The young man peeped over the top of the lace fan he was waggling rapidly before his face and fluttered his eyelashes at us. "Hello," he said, coyly.

Butch and I looked at each other in total astonishment. It felt as if we were trapped in some bad movie and the whole audience was just laughing their heads off at our expense. We both murmured our hellos, and I gave the young fellow a feeble smile. Since that first experience I've learned that teen gays often like to employ shock tactics just to test adults' acceptance level. I think it has more to do with being a teenager than with being gay.

On the way back to Sunnyside, Bruce talked animatedly nonstop about his experience at the meeting. His spirit, which a few short days earlier had seemed all but broken, had revived. Like Lazarus raised from the dead, my son was coming back to life.

By the next meeting, however, my gut was fighting back again and all the old trepidations had returned, this time with a brutal vengeance. Bruce had been telling me about the particularly bad day he had at school, and I felt totally exhausted from my lack of sleep and the struggle that roared on like a devastating cyclone inside of me. Butch did not go with us this time, and I was driving along a particularly dangerous and winding stretch of road. Up ahead I saw a sharp curve approaching. At the very top of this curve stood a massive oak tree. How easy it would be to put an end to all this, I suddenly considered, and the notion was at once very beguiling. The car hurtled toward the curve as my foot eased down still further on the accelerator. The telephone poles and fence posts were already rushing past in a blur when I noticed the speedometer jump five miles per hour, then ten. My hands gripped the steering wheel tightly. I felt as though I were suddenly free-falling through time and space. Everything vanished except that oak tree dead ahead. My mind was consumed with the idea that sweet release, for both me and my son, lay at the bottom of that big tree. All I had to do was let it happen when I reached the curve, now no more than thirty yards away, and then . . . oblivion.

I do not know what power lifted my foot off that accelerator or made my hands rotate the steering wheel away from the tree. I only know that I did somehow negotiate the curve safely, though the tears were streaming down my face. What a vile and horrible vision had passed before me! I was benumbed by this brush with absolute evil. What right had I even to consider taking the life of my son? Like Abraham, I had been conducting my son down the road to Moriah, and that oak tree had almost become the altar where I would have sacrificed him. I had somehow convinced myself that this was a desirable alternative to life as a gay person.

"Are you all right, mom?" Bruce asked, placing his hand on top of mine.

Looking at him, I could see the deep concern in his eyes, along with some of the old fear and sadness. I felt so ashamed for having entertained such truly wicked schemes and indeed for having risked my dear son's life as well as my own. "Bruce, honey," I said, trying weakly to smile to reassure him. "You are not responsible for my feelings. — I am. Have faith in me until I can work my way through this."

The next morning, standing before my bathroom mirror, I took a long, hard look at the haggard woman who stood there looking back accusingly at me. A few days earlier I had gone, in the middle of the afternoon, to our empty church and literally thrown myself prostrate upon the floor before the altar, desperately beseeching God to take this burden from me. All I got in return for this dramatic performance was ear-splitting silence. I was becoming almost angry with God. But then, as I stood there in the humble surroundings of my tiny bathroom, regarding my own pathetic reflection in the glass, a small voice did begin to whisper to me. God was breaking his silence at last, not in booming grandiloquence with flourishes of trumpets and crashing cymbals, but in a small, calm and gentle whisper: "Child," said the voice. "Why must you keep trying to place your hateful, ugly stereotypes of gay people onto the face of your beloved son like some hideous mask? The face of the gay community *is* the face of your son. You really *do* know what a gay person is like. After all, you've lived with one for over thirteen years now. He is the same boy in which you have always taken such delight."

An enlightenment had come upon me. In an instant the world began to make a little more sense. This was something I could understand, and understanding, better than anything else, quiets fear. I could feel transformation overtaking my life like the Phoenix reconstituting itself from the ashes of its former existence.

After my bathroom revelation I never shed another tear over the fact that my son is gay, though I have indeed shed many tears because of the outrageous indignities and injustices suffered by Bruce, and hundreds of thousands of other gay people, at the hands of an ignorant and intolerant society. I still had much to learn, but I'd come through my first trial by fire intact, if not unscathed.

*

*   *

PFLAG is the national organization of Parents and Friends of Lesbians and Gays. Though the organization is involved in many activities, its basic function is that of support group. We attended our first meeting in Louisville, Kentucky just a few weeks after Bruce's coming out to us.

The meeting was held in the study of one member's home. We sat in a semicircle and each one introduced themselves in turn. My God, I thought, did that woman just say she was the parent of *two* gay children?! She said it so matter-of-factly! And this good-looking young guy here next to me, did he really say, "I am the gay son of heterosexual parents?" Everyone laughed at his remark except me. That hit a little too close to home, and I wasn't at the point yet where I could view such remarks as funny. When it came my turn I blurted out that our thirteen-year-old son had just told his heterosexual parents he was gay, whereupon I immediately dissolved into tears. The young man sitting next to me immediately apologized for having been so flip. Later, two other young gay men knelt in front of me and, holding my hands, told me it was all right to cry. They said they loved me just for being there.

And cry I most certainly did, though these were different tears now. They were tears of release, as hope was being born in my heart. I could see my son's face reflected in the faces of these caring young men. I saw families who were there together, each one supporting the others. They were farther down the road than I had yet come. Sure, I heard stories of adversity and opposition, but I also heard stories of courage, triumph and hope.

Suddenly I had a whole room full of role models, people to inspire me and ideals to aspire to. When we broke up into smaller discussion groups, I told the other mothers in my group that I wanted to get to the point where they had arrived. One said to me she thought the heart of a true activist beat within my breast. Yeah, right, I thought. That's about the funniest thing I've ever heard. They said it was remarkable I had come to a PFLAG meeting so soon after learning my child was gay. Usually it takes a lot longer for people to overcome their fear and embarrassment. I didn't tell them about my bathroom revelation, and all that had gone before it, still being too shy and afraid of sounding ridiculous.

Much to my amazement, my heart was singing on the trip back home from Louisville. I couldn't wait until the next meeting, but that was a very long month away. How could I bear the waiting?

As it turned out, our vacation that year would supersede the June PFLAG meeting. Our plans to stay at a family resort in Myrtle Beach had been long in the making, and there was nothing to do but go through with them. But because of my new-found sensitivity to the realities of gay life, this vacation provided me with an unforeseen opportunity to learn.

Shortly after arriving, I began to notice how Bruce seemed just as isolated and alone there as he did at home. All the other teens were busy heing and sheing, pairing up down on the beach while Bruce spent most of his time alone sitting atop a sand dune staring at the sea. It appeared there were to be no summer crushes for him, and if there were, he'd best keep them to himself. It was clear that my son was to be denied what other kids considered, if they even thought about it at all, simply to be a part of being young, their birthright, if you will.

One afternoon, while having lunch at a nearby restaurant, I noticed a handsome blond teenager enter with his family. He looked to be about Bruce's age and, as I sat there munching my French fries, I could see that this strapping youth had not gone unnoticed by my son. What's more, the strapping youth was casting more than a few casual glances in Bruce's direction as well. I was fascinated! Clearly they were flirting. There was no other word for it. I leaned over and whispered in Bruce's ear, "He likes you, too." He grinned shyly, obviously basking in the attention. More scales had fallen from my eyes. A world I had been totally blind to was starting to reveal itself. What other aspects of Bruce's life had ignorance and prejudice blinded me to?

This occurrence sensitized me to certain gay behavior that other straight people simply missed altogether. Like the two men shopping in the supermarket on a Sunday morning back in Sunnyside. They both had arm baskets, but took off in opposite directions. Presently, they would meet surreptitiously in a side aisle to compare their gathered goods with their common shopping list. Obviously they were going to rather great lengths to conceal the fact that they were together. One noticed I was wearing an AIDS ribbon (one of my first small acts of courage in Sunnyside). He approached me looking at my ribbon. Suddenly he glanced up and our eyes met. "Thanks," he whispered, and quickly disappeared down the next aisle and back into his secret life.

CHAPTER

VII

I was eager to attend my next PFLAG meeting. Since we were all still very much "in the closet" back in Sunnyside, it was just about the only time of the month when I felt really free and alive. I quickly came to understand the toll that a life in the closet exacts upon those who feel they must live it. In Sunnyside, I avoided family and friends for months, even those few close friends to whom I had confided my suspicions before I knew for certain that Bruce was gay. I didn't know who, if anyone, could be trusted and was afraid to take the risk. Things for Bruce were already bad enough at school. I didn't want some vicious, wildcat rumor to make them any worse.

It was from friends in the Louisville chapter that I found out about the PFLAG group in Bloomington. This chapter met on a different day of the month from the one in Kentucky. I was overjoyed to learn that it was possible for me to actually receive a much-needed second monthly shot in the arm by also joining the Bloomington chapter, which I promptly did. Bruce had also joined the gay youth group in Louisville. So, with our affiliations in both cities we were now traveling about 500 miles per month to attend meetings, and sometimes as much as 1,000 miles if there were special events in addition to the meetings themselves. This is a pretty good indication of just how important the support we were receiving was to us and to our son.

We were now living two separate lives, our hidden life with our new friends in Bloomington and Louisville and our fearful, closeted life in Sunnyside. Our absences were becoming more and more difficult to explain to our friends, especially at church. They didn't understand why we seemed to be out of town so much of the time. We told them we were spending time with family, and it really didn't feel like a lie. We had developed a bond with many of the people at PFLAG that felt like "family," and simply did not exist anywhere else for us at the time.

Our active participation at church continued, however, and we went on attending regularly. If anything, I felt my faith had been tested and made stronger by recent events. At this point it still would have been for me utterly impossible to envision the ordeal that lay ahead for us.

*

*   *

Several years earlier, when our congregation had needed to find a replacement for Pastor Saunders, I was asked to serve on the search and nominating committee along with eight other church members. We worked hard for many months, and developed a blind filing system whereby we could pick applicants without regard to race, age or gender. But the search did not go well, and we were becoming discouraged by the long, fruitless hours of work we had put in. Finally, we were able to narrow the field to just three candidates, a middle-aged Scottish pastor, a middle-aged woman and a young associate pastor. When word got out that one of the candidates was a woman, she was immediately eliminated by a powerful cadre of a few influential traditionalist members who disguised their gender bias behind the assumption that our congregation was not "ready" for a woman pastor to lead it. So much for the blind filing system we had worked so meticulously to develop and maintain.

We interviewed the Scottish pastor and the young associate. It became readily apparent very early on that the Scotsman had already chosen another position, and he had a lot of fun toying with what he undoubtedly viewed as a bunch of small-town rubes. This left us with young Mark Roberts as our only candidate.

Roberts didn't sit too well with me. For one thing he had managed to circumvent the blind filing system and directly approached two other female members of the committee privately. Mark easily charmed the women into becoming enthusiastic supporters of him, while I considered his behavior nothing short of unethical. Other conservative members of the committee refused the moderator's request that Mark's name be placed in the blind filing system. So, the game of congregational politics, which we had tried so hard to avoid, had clearly become the determining factor in the process of nominating our new spiritual leader.

I was assigned the job of checking on Mark's background and calling his references. The very first reference I contacted gave him considerably less than a glowing recommendation. This, of course, only served to intensify my misgivings. His youth and inexperience were of some concern to me, but I also quickly came to believe that the real motivation behind his somewhat Machiavellian manipulations to get himself appointed our pastor was not because of some deeply religious "calling," but arose merely out of a desire to be back in Indiana where he and his wife would be closer to their home towns and families. This was, of course, an understandable desire on Mark's part, but hardly ranked, in my estimation at least, as a significant motive for a man's wanting to become the spiritual guide of a congregation of several hundred people. The moderator of the committee knew I was struggling with Mark's impending nomination. She suggested to me that his maturity level probably matched that of the congregation as a whole, and perhaps they could grow together.

In the end, the two women whom Mark had co-opted had begun to have some second thoughts of their own about him. Mostly out of a desire to reach a decision before the committee disintegrated completely, however, we decided to call Rev. Mark Roberts as our pastor. There was no way I could have foreseen at the time the direct consequences his selection would eventually have upon my life and family.

Very early on in his tenure I began to sense in Mark an abiding hostility toward me. Later I learned that one of his allies on the nominating committee had communicated my apprehensions to him. This was a great betrayal of trust, as the conversations and deliberations that took place among committee members were supposed to remain strictly confidential.

Many church members complained that our new pastor seemed arrogant and unapproachable. It was a difficult adjustment, especially since our interim pastor had been such a warm, loving and gentle man. More than a few wanted him to remain as our permanent minister, but Presbyterian church law forbids that.

The real impact of our mistake did not hit home, however, until one Sunday morning when Rev. Roberts declared from the pulpit that he believed the majority of the congregation, with only a few exceptions, to be good conservative Republicans like himself. I was stunned. I had never in my life heard a minister make declarations of political preference from the pulpit, nor intimate that one party was better than another. We "few exceptions" were deeply shocked and offended by such a conspicuous attempt on the part of our pastor to alienate us from the rest of our church family through the use of national partisan politics.

At eleven years old, my son was then rapidly approaching the age when he could formally join the church, and he expressed a strong desire to do so. Bruce's wish to become a Presbyterian must have been quite unshakable, especially when I consider now that he was willing to endure the disdain of Rev. Roberts during his confirmation classes. Mark mentioned to me, and to Bruce as well, on several occasions that he thought Bruce was "different," that he was "soft." Such remarks were often accompanied by a facial expression of great distaste, as though the pastor had just caught a whiff of some foul odor.

It was about this same time that the General Assembly of the Presbyteran Church decided to refuse the recommendations of its own Commission on Human Sexuality by denying gays full access to the life of the church. I remember hearing the men in the back row at choir rehearsal making remarks about how we had "kept the queers out." It filled me with apprehension to think that my son was about to be confirmed into a church that would ostracize him if he were gay. At the time, I literally shuddered to imagine what might happen if my darkest fears were realized (that Bruce was in fact gay) and those men in the back row of the choir ever discovered it.

One evening, just prior to Bruce's coming out to me, I received a distressed phone call from a woman in our congregation whom I greatly admired. I was immediately concerned because she sounded so upset. I told her I'd be right over, and immediately jumped into the car and drove to her home. Sitting directly across the kitchen table from her, I could see the pain and anxiety in her eyes. She was very much afraid of what she was about to tell me. After a very slow, deep breath she said: "Rhea, I'm gay."

A calmness that I had neither expected nor experienced before settled over me at once. "But, I like you for you," I replied quietly. "It just doesn't matter." And then, seemingly from out of nowhere, I somehow gathered the courage to tell her that in my heart I believed Bruce to be gay too.

I have never forgotten the look of relief that came over her face. It was like a combination of joy, release and gratefulness all rolled into one. We talked long into the night, and from then on, for the next several weeks, she was one of my main sources of information about what it meant to be gay. I must have driven her crazy with all my questions. But she was very kind and helpful, and strongly encouraged me to let Bruce evolve on his own, advising me that if he truly was gay it would eventually emerge. Above all, however, she believed Bruce must be self-identified. I agreed with her then, and I still do.

Perhaps it was just my growing awareness, or maybe the increased visibility of gay people in the news at the time, but I began to notice more and more homophobic comments at church. I often thought of the friend who had confided her homosexuality to me in the days and weeks that followed Bruce's own coming out. She was enormously liked and respected by her fellow church members. How would they feel, I wondered, if they knew her secret? Would it make a difference? Could they adjust and accept her? What about my son? I can see now that the answer to that question was much closer to me than I could ever have foreseen at the time. The die had most certainly been inalterably cast by then.

*
*   *

I believe strongly that the minister sets the tone of the parish. It is unavoidable. If the pastor is open to people, willing and able to accept their humanity and to love them for it (rather than in spite of it) then those attributes are bound to be reflected in the life of the parish. If, on the other hand, the pastor is of a closed-minded and judg- mental nature, with a narrow view of mankind and our potential for goodness, then the life of his congregation will be cast into that frame of reference.

One Sunday Rev. Roberts decided to use his sermon as an opportunity to single out for ridicule a particular men's conference that had gained the national media's attention at the time. He talked about how they sat around "beating on their drums." He made fun of the meeting's agenda, which he read aloud, ridiculing each item as though he were some stand-up comedian, elicit- ing much laughter from the congregation. "Oh, yes, and my personal favorite," he said, stifling his own guffaws,

"Dialogue with Gay Men." At that point he, along with much of the congregation, dissolved once again into uproarious laughter.

But I wasn't laughing, and I could feel the heat rising in my cheeks, as I sat in my place in the choir loft. Why was the very idea of straight men having a dialogue with gay men supposed to be so funny? Amid all the hoots and laughter, my gaze fell upon one of the church's beautiful stained-glass windows. It was my favorite, and I would often look at it during the service, especially when the sun shown through its multicolored panels, casting a warm, rainbow glow over everything and everyone inside the sanctuary, just as it did that morning. It was a depiction of Christ with the little children. "Suffer the little children to come unto me." I turned the verse over in my mind, and as I did so a strange, sickening feeling came upon me. *Yeah, all except my child*, I suddenly thought, and the realization hit me like a physical blow. In my heart I whispered a desperate prayer that my son might somehow miraculously escape the terrible stigma of being gay. It was a prayer I would repeat countless times over and over for the now numbered Sunday mornings that would remain for me to continue to occupy my place in the choir.

I began hearing rumors about ugly Session meetings (the Session is the council of church elders that constitutes the governing body of each individual Presbyterian church) where one member had dared to suggest that gay people were also the children of God and should not be singled out for exclusion from the church. For this opinion she was literally labeled the Antichrist by another Session member, who stood up and screamed his accusations at her from across the room.

Bruce's emotional acknowledgement to me of his homosexuality had already taken place by the time these frightening stories began reaching my ears. Clearly, a widening gulf was developing between us and our church family. They were completely oblivious of the tremendous, painful wounds they were inflicting upon me with their

ss comments and their stupidly malicious igno-
ll, I continued to serve the church and attended
but of course felt forced to carefully conceal my
s the mother of a gay child.

To me it is still the greatest irony of my life that when the day finally did arrive that Bruce came out to me, when I could no longer ignore the fact that he was gay, my relationship with the church actually made it more difficult for me to adjust, rather than less so. For it was there, among this congregation of good people, of good *Christian* people, that I first experienced the depth of ignorance, the loathing and the hostility my son would have to face in life simply for being who he is. When Bruce, Butch and I most needed the support, understanding and fellowship of our church family, they could not be there for us. We were cast out, and had to face a world of hatred and hostility alone. It was a devastating blow from which I still have not fully recovered. I'm not sure I ever shall.

At a choir rehearsal, one wintry Wednesday evening in early 1993 (several months after Bruce's coming out to his family), conversation turned to the issue of gays in the military. It was a discussion that Rev. Roberts joined in on with whole-hearted conviction. He assumed the same mockingly supercilious attitude that he had exhibited during the sermon about the men's conference. After Mark left the room someone told a joke that clearly demeaned gay people. I found this offensive and felt extremely embarrassed and uncomfortable. I knew I could not go home and look my boy in the eye if I let that joke go by unchallenged. I mustered all my courage and told the would-be comedian that I didn't think he had a very Christ-like attitude. I said that I had several gay friends that I cared about very much, and didn't appreciate such derisive "fun" at their expense.

At once the group burst into a brouhaha of chatter. I was shocked and, in truth, deeply frightened by the change that came over those people, most of whom a split second before I had counted among my dearest friends. Many of their faces assumed a disgusted ugliness I would never before have considered them capable of. Someone said that gays deserved our contempt because they caused AIDS. I responded that I thought AIDS was caused by a non-discriminating virus. Another said her husband would not even permit the subject of homosexuality to be discussed in their house because he despised gays so. The choir director stated flatly that the gays she had known all had very tragic and unhappy lives. Self-denial was the only real option for them, she said, just like alcoholics. I still wish I had had the courage to say that Bruce is gay and that when you say those awful things you're talking about my son. But I hadn't yet gathered that kind of pluck.

Following the rehearsal I hurried to the home of my close friend, Dixie Beer, whose back door was just across the alley from the church. I literally collapsed in a flood of tears that I simply could no longer keep dammed up inside. Dixie was originally from Cincinnati and had several gay friends there. Knowing this, I had recently risked taking her into my confidence, telling her the whole truth. She comforted me as best she could, but I was near total hysteria.

For many days following the incident at choir rehearsal I couldn't seem to stop myself from suddenly just bursting into tears. All self-control seemed to have deserted me. I kept seeing those awful faces, twisted as they were by raw, unrestrained hatred. Still, I couldn't believe that these were really bad people — ignorant and frightened, yes, but not bad. In a way, this even made things worse. But it was abundantly clear, however, that something basic had been changed by the events of that night, and I would never be able to see those people in the same way again. I felt devastated, weak and exhausted. I did receive a letter from the choir director apologizing for allowing the situation to become so heated and to get out of hand. Otherwise, there was no apology from anyone for their general ugliness toward me. I made up my mind I had to go back. I had to face them. It was very difficult and awkward that first Sunday following the choir-practice episode. I could feel people staring at me as I sat in my place in the choir loft. But I was there to prove a point, that I wasn't afraid of their stares or their whispers.

The scripture that Sunday was from the second chapter of James, verses 12-13. "Speak and act as those who are going to be judged by the law that gives freedom, because judgement without mercy will be shown to anyone who has not been merciful. Mercy triumphs over judgement!" Of course, no one present, especially Rev. Roberts himself, could have imagined how much this passage of scripture had come to mean to me in the days directly preceding that Sunday morning service. God had surely revealed his presence to me through the words of St. James.

*

* *

Despite our efforts to keep up appearances until the commotion simmered down, from the choir-rehearsal incident onward things quickly got progressively worse. Members of the choir reported the episode to Rev. Roberts, whereupon he speculated openly, apparently to anyone who would listen, that I was sensitive to the subject of homosexuality because Bruce was in fact gay. This was in essence, if not in fact, tantamount to my son's being outed by his own pastor to the congregation. We first got wind of this situation from my friend Dixie after Mark came to her with his conjectures concerning Bruce's sexual orientation. He finally actually asked her point blank whether she knew if Bruce was in fact gay. She informed Rev. Roberts that that was a subject he had best take up with the Murray family and not with anyone else.

Before departing Dixie's home, Mark told her he had already talked it over with several other members of the congregation, and all agreed they believed Bruce to be gay. At that point Dixie informed him of her intention to make us aware of his actions, feeling that we should have the opportunity to prepare ourselves for the worst. Surprised by Dixie's candor, Mark left without another word.

Of course the small-town rumor mill immediately went into high gear, and it wasn't long before the whole community was talking about "that queer Murray kid." The version that made its way back to us was that Bruce must be gay; after all even his own pastor said so.

Upon learning about the conversation between Dixie and Mark, Butch called Rev. Roberts from work and, with a restraint born of a desire to behave as he believed Christ would have him, told Mark that he had deeply wounded our family through his gross lack of professionalism and common human decency. He asked the pastor how he would like it if someone started unkind and harmful rumors circulating around the community about his own son.

Mark apologized profusely, and thanked Butch for his calm and "Christ-like" attitude. He admitted that such a response would have been beyond him. I'm sure, for once, Mark's reply came straight from the heart, since my husband is built like an NFL fullback and could easily have cleaned house with the callow young pastor had he chosen to do so.

Within less than an hour of Butch's phone call, Mark was standing on our front doorstep. When I let him in he immediately collapsed into a chair and began to weep. The first words out of his mouth were, "I shouldn't be a minister." He told me he didn't know how to relate to people nor how to empathize with them. He knew he came across as cold and distant, incapable of intimacy. I felt he was being sincere. I believed he was at the brink of a moment of personal truth, insight similar to the self-revelation I had experience before my bathroom mirror several months earlier. He was there, on the very verge, but he decided to back away. I could see it happening. He simply could not bear the sight of his own reflection, as it were, so he turned away from it. In an instant his attitude had changed. Now, with dry-eyed aplomb, he indicated that the reason he had said what he had to Dixie was only out of pastoral concern for us. He was just trying to figure out a way to reach us, to be helpful.

I had been very distraught prior to Mark's arrival, but God's presence was with me and had a cooling and calming affect on my emotions. I told Mark frankly that it was true that Bruce was gay. I began to explain what I had learned from the experience of coming to terms with my son's sexual orientation, about exploding the stereotypical myths about gays by simply putting the face of my child on the gay community. I told him how disappointed I was in the church's response to the plight of gay people and their families. But I carefully explained though I felt abandoned by the church, I had not been abandoned by God. The unconditional love I had been seeking in the church I had finally found in PFLAG. I asked him why AIDS patients were not being ministered to by the church instead of being treated like modern-day lepers. Didn't the church remember how Christ had treated the lepers? I asked him what had happened to the love and compassion of Jesus when it came to the church's ministering to people with AIDS.

His response was that the church feared us (gay people, their friends and families), and that he doubted we would ever be able to find a church that would welcome and accept us. To this I replied that the most frequent injunction in the Bible was "Fear not." Didn't Christ teach us that love drives out all fear?

In the end Mark said something about standing in awe of me and that I had obviously had a "burning-bush experience." I had the feeling he was almost envious of the insights my recent experience had given me, insights that his fear would never permit him even the opportunity to grasp.

I reminded him of how he had treated Bruce in the past. Mark hung his head and admitted he had indeed been unkind and thoughtless toward my son.

Before departing my house he told me that he really had no idea exactly how many people in the congregation he had speculated about Bruce's homosexuality to. He then returned to Dixie for another tearful, emotional exchange. The next day he came once more to our house and apologized to Bruce, who forgave him unconditionally.

At the high school, where my son was in the midst of his freshman year, all hell broke loose (and I mean that in a very real sense). Where there had once been only speculation concerning Bruce's homosexuality, there now appeared to be incontrovertible proof, courtesy of Rev. Roberts. Where there had once been mostly taunts and verbal harassment, there was now open, aggressive physical hostility. Bruce was spit upon, kicked, hit, beaten up, verbally humiliated, and had his property vandalized. These acts often took place in full view of faculty members and administrators, who stood by and did nothing, sometimes even seemingly amused. Once another student, screaming the word "abomination," actually slammed the Bible into the side of Bruce's head so hard it knocked him down. There were also numerous death threats. My son was living in an unrelenting nightmare of terror that no adult could ever fully imagine without experiencing it. Comparisons to some of the dehumanizing torment suffered by the Jews just prior to the holocaust do not significantly stretch credibility. But this was happening right here in America in the 1990s, not somewhere in Nazi Germany during the mid 1930s.

Once, in the locker room after physical education, for example, Bruce suddenly found himself surrounded by five boys. They told him he had better not let them catch him out alone, because if they did they would rape, torture and kill him and then dump his body in a ditch. They gave every indication that they were deadly serious about their intentions.

Needless to say, our double life was now no more. Regardless of what else happened to us we could not, indeed would not, return to our closet of fear. In a very real sense we had been liberated and were now able to speak our truth openly for ourselves. In the end, nearly nine months of living a dreadfully dishonest existence had taught me that it was not the kind of life I wanted for myself nor for my son. For him I wanted a life of integrity, empowerment, self-respect, personal fulfillment and joy, in short, the kind of life that can only be lived in the light of day and not in some dark closet, suffocating in shame.

Butch and I on our wedding day (April 25, 1976).

Butch reads a bedtime story to Tanya and Bruce (about 1982).

Christmas at the Murray home during happier times (about 1988).

Gripped by sheer terror, I mount the podium once
again (1996).

CHAPTER VIII

The months spent in the closet comprised the longest relentlessly difficult period of my life. The amount of energy that it took to maintain the constant façade of calm, "normal" respectability robbed my life of all its joy and pleasure and in their place gave me only fear and suspicion. Everyone I met, old friend or mere acquaintance, was a potential Judas. I felt I could trust no one. Every day presented a new struggle of delicately balancing the truth with hundreds of carefully constructed little deceptions. I had always taught my kids that one of the most serious wrongs they could commit was to tell a lie. Yet here I was, virtually living one myself, compromising the truth at every turn.

My heart ached for the lost intimacy of friends and family, even as I meticulously avoided them. Of course this in itself caused many to suspect there was something amiss. They asked questions that would often require rather elaborate fabricated responses. I hated deceiving them even in little ways, but I was so afraid of what might happen to Bruce, and to the rest of us, should they discover the truth. I had seen how good and kindly people could turn mean and hateful at the mere mention of the word "gay."

Well founded though my fears might have been, there came a time when they had to be faced and dealt with. The idea of living out the rest of life in a kind of semi-isolation was not an attractive prospect to a basically congenial person like me, who enjoys the company of friends and family. Finally the day arrived when I decided to go to my mother.

My parents had mellowed considerably in their later years as life had become less of a struggle for them. We had spent many hours dealing with the painful issues that had divided us from each other in the past. My mother, father and I had all been working very hard to forge a new, closer relationship. I didn't want to jeopardize this hard-won intimacy by unloading problems on them they simply could not cope with. I knew my mother suspected something was wrong. I could read concern in her deep, violet-blue eyes. But every time I thought of telling her, my fear would bring me up short.

Bruce had a very close bond with his grandmother. They would often have little dates together to go shopping or for ice cream. He delighted in pampering her and would often spend the evening at my parents' home. I remember how proud he was when I brought her to his school for lunch on Parents' Day. I knew that mother was apprehensive about appearing at the school. She was always very self-conscious about what she considered to be her facial deformity. She feared the children's ridicule, or that their derision might be transferred to her grandson. In Bruce's eyes, however, she was nothing short of gorgeous, and he beamed when he saw us enter the room. His obvious love and pride in his grandmother soon melted away all her anxieties, allowing her to fully enjoy herself.

I set out for mother's house on that fateful afternoon determined to unburden my soul to her. When I got there, however, I fell once again into the same old chatty, small-talk routine I had been using for weeks in order to avoid talking about what was really on my mind.

Suddenly she reached across the table and took my hand, stopping me in mid-banality. "Rhea, honey," she implored. "What's bothering you? I can tell something has been eating you alive for quite some time now. You know a mother can always tell when one of her children is hurting."

I sat there just staring at her, unable to speak and feeling the tears welling up in my eyes. "Now tell me, darling," she continued softly. "Is it something to do with our Bruce?" She regarded me intently. "Tell me," she reiterated, after a moment's silence. "Is he gay?" And, with her sixth-grade education she added: "I hope you know that I love Bruce even if he is a 'heterosexual'."

I had to smile. "I think you mean 'homosexual'. Yes, mama, it's true. Bruce is gay," I said, astonished as the realization began to dawn that she had already guessed the truth.

My mother took me in her arms and, as she kissed away my tears, she also banished from my heart the scars of my childhood. So, that which I had feared would wreak destruction upon my newly emerging intimacy with my mother had, in fact, become a vehicle for continued healing. Given our background and limited experience, I never could have imagined this would have turned out to be the case. There appeared to me no other explanation for this happy outcome except God's grace.

Later that same day, mother broke the news to my father. Amazingly, he was not in the least surprised. Dad said that from the time Bruce was five or six years old he had felt certain his grandson was gay. Like mom, my dad's response could not have been more positive and supportive.

What is perhaps even more astounding is that neither of my parents had any intention of just learning the truth and then sweeping the whole thing under the rug, as is often the case with family members. They intended to participate fully in my son's life as a gay person. My father, for example, would often ask Bruce how his love life was in the same way he might ask a straight grandson that question, with the full expectation of an honest response. A year later, his grandparents would invite Bruce to bring his date for a gay prom (sponsored by the Indianapolis chapter of IYG) by the house so they could meet him. They treated this occasion exactly as they did when Tanya attended a school dance, with photographs and good wishes.

My mom and dad rallied around us and climbed right into the trenches. I remember how strongly my mother reacted against all the nasty gossip in town, and I still can hear her railing about the way we had been abandoned by the church. Her own bitter past experience allowed her readily to identify with Bruce's cruel and unjust rejection by society. She found she could fight for her grandson even though her own diffidence precluded her standing up to those who had humiliated her in the past. Hers was a courage truly born of love. As poverty and adversity had brought out the worst in my parents many years earlier, their involvement in Bruce's struggle seemed to bring out the best.

Unfortunately, the response of my husband's family to the news that Bruce was gay was a far more typical one.

Frequently, on Sundays, the entire Murray clan would gather at the home of Butch's sister, Marcia. These close family occasions were filled with much warmth and laughter. I took great pleasure in the fact that my sister-in-law was also such a dear friend to me. When one of us was facing a personal crisis, we would always call up the other and say, "It's cookies-and-milk time." It was a standing joke with us that rather than crying into our beer, we cried into our cookies and milk. We would take day trips to historical Madison, Indiana, where we would spend more time just sitting and talking on a park bench by the Ohio River than seeing the sights. We shared our hopes and our dreams as well as our fears with a complete understanding and confidence in each other born of deep mutual trust.

But Marcia, like some others among our friends and family, had begun to pull away from Bruce as he grew older. This gradual distancing became more and more apparent as invitations to Marcia's home began to dwindle. If there were family birthday parties, we would receive last minute invitations that prior commitments made it difficult or impossible for us to accept. We were invited to Thanksgiving dinner and then had the invitation rescinded because Marcia said she was having a fight with her husband. Later, through a slip of the tongue, we found out that the invitation had been canceled only for us. Butch and I came to believe that the reason for this obvious shunning was Bruce. As it turned out, there had always been sneering whispers among my husband's family about Bruce being gay from the time he was a small boy. When he neared puberty, however, such conjecturing intensified, taking on a kind of reality of its own, and causing many to withdraw from him.

During our time in the closet, like others among our friends and family, Marcia had become suspicious that something was up. She called me one afternoon convinced that Butch and I were on the brink of getting a divorce. I saw this as an opportunity to clear the air and told her frankly that Bruce was gay. She seemed almost relieved by this, but was particularly concerned about her brother's reaction. I told her that Butch loved his son and was standing behind him one hundred percent. Marcia said that she loved Bruce too, and that in fact the rest of the family already knew, so there was no need for me to tell them. I was concerned about Marcia's son, Jason, since he was one of the very few friends Bruce still had left. She told me not to mention it to him, that she would sit Jason down and have a talk with him about it.

From that moment, a curtain of silence, which has rarely been breached since, descended between us and my husband's family. Our relationship with them became superficial, awkward, often very tense. This was especially true with Marcia and me. I kept waiting for a sign of acceptance and understanding, but it never came. Those dwindling invitations became rarer still, and our isolation from Butch's family, with the exception of his mother, was nearly complete.

The one happy outcome of this situation was Jason's response. As it turned out, for whatever reasons of her own, Marcia had not said a word to him. I'm not sure she ever intended to. From remarks that Jason made in Bruce's presence, I came to realize that he did not know. Once, during a visit to our house, Bruce and I finally broke the news.

"Aw, come on, son," he said, in his low-key, country-boy way. "You're puttin' me on. You're smilin', I see. I know you're pullin' my leg."

The completely open, unaffected sincerity that emanated from Jason's handsome, honest face elicited a burst of charmed laughter from Bruce and me. "No, no, Jason," Bruce said, trying his best to be serious. "It's true. I am totally gay."

"Well," he replied, with a shy smile and a shrug of his broad shoulders. "That's cool. You're still Bruce, ain't ya'?"

Jason has never exhibited anything but complete acceptance, and he remains one of Bruce's most loyal and trusted friends.

It's hard to grow up and live your life in an intolerant and suspicious community without some of those characteristics rubbing off on you, and Marcia was probably no exception. Butch used to half-jokingly say: "I come from a family of equal opportunity bigots. They hate everybody." Words like nigger, kike, spic and fag tumbled from their lips like so much water over Niagara Falls, (though they would often tone down their rhetoric around me, knowing of my extreme dislike of such pejorative language). Disparaging remarks about anyone considered "different" comprised the subject matter of much of the family's stock conversation. I believe that Marcia felt her brother truly shared these negative values, but that I had influenced him to behave to the contrary. After all, they had both been exposed to the same poisons as children. Butch, however, was and is altogether his own man. The time he spent in Southeast Asia, though a grim experience in most ways, provided him the opportunity to get away from southern Indiana and encounter other viewpoints, other worlds and other peoples. It can truly be said that Butch's home-grown prejudices were among the very few propitious casualties of the Vietnam war. The starvation and suffering of Vietnamese children, brought on by a senseless war, were more than his heart could bear. It made an indelible impression that often troubles him yet. He would sometimes spend his entire pay on food, which he then distributed among the families of villages near to where he was stationed. Unable to stop, because of the danger from Vietcong snipers, he would drive quickly through a village, flinging parcels of food from his jeep as he went. "Gooks" was not a word he would ever have applied to the people of Vietnam, and he did not take kindly to those who did.

Butch also shared a hootch (a kind of prefabricated, movable barracks) with several African-Americans. In the heat of battle, the color of the man's skin who is fighting next to you suddenly doesn't matter much. It's whether you can count on him or not that's important. Butch learned he had to be there for his black buddies if he was going to expect the same of them, and that meant outside the foxhole as well as in. His Vietman experience gave him a healthy respect, a compassion and a positive regard for all humanity. It was his kindness, openness and generosity of spirit toward virtually everyone that caused me to fall in love with him in the first place. Knowing, as I do, the kind of childhood conditioning and socialization he had to conquer in order to become the man he is today makes him that much more exceptional, and indeed attractive, in my eyes.

*
*   *

I quickly came to realize that coming out of the closet was not just one big event in a person's life. It was more of an on-going kind of experience. After opening up to my parents and to Marcia, I began to think about all the people in my life who still didn't know. It appeared as though our lives from now on would be comprised of an endless series of anxious traumas. Every new acquaintanceship brought new doubts and misgivings as to when and whether to come out. Naturally enough, this causes tensions and anxieties, which can become burdensome to any relationship. Should we tell right away, or should we wait until we know the person better? But, if we wait, does that indicate we feel we have something to hide, like some deep, dark, shameful secret? That certainly wouldn't leave a favorable impression. Still, timing seemed to be of crucial importance. Butch and I often speculated, late at night, as to who would stand by us and who would not. After some experience, however, we decided this was a useless exercise. There is absolutely no fool-proof way of predicting how people are going to react to homosexuality itself or to one's expressions of positive feelings about it. Some who we believed would be totally reasonable were the first to denounce us, while others we thought would never understand remained steadfast and loyal.

There is also what I call "the first-wave/second-wave phenomenon." Sometimes people whose initial reaction seems altogether supportive will quickly back away from you after thinking things over. On the other hand, there are also those who react quite negatively at first, but then later, with time for reflection, can become your greatest supporters. This is why it is so very important to always try to keep lines of communication open. People really can change, and often it's for the better. Those who change for the worse may someday come back around as well.

As I pondered my list of friends and relations, two people stood out, and their potential reactions weighed heavily upon my thoughts. These were my close friend, Nancy, and my daughter, Tanya. I treasured dearly my relationship with Nancy, and I knew any kind of a "Sophie's choice" between my children would be unbearable and impossible for me. I had heard that the ones you are the closest to are the ones you tell last, and it certainly turned out to be true in my case.

I was certain that Nancy loved Bruce beyond any shadow of a possible doubt. She had been involved in his life even before he was born, and always said he was especially chosen by God to do wonderful things. Nancy and I would often get together on Mondays to talk, not just chit-chat but to share our thoughts and, often, bare our battered souls. We never feared judgement or rejection from one another. Perhaps I should have had more faith in her than I did, in this particular case. Many times I came close to telling her, but then some mean-sounding, thoughtless remark on her part would remind me that Nancy was also a product of the same old intolerant upbringing so ubiquitous throughout our little community, and I would keep my silence. I could almost hear my closet door slamming shut as I hastily withdrew back into the darkness.

Eventually, however, I came to realize that, by threatening our intimacy, my very silence itself was pushing me steadily toward the brink of losing Nancy anyway. What difference did it make in the end if our friendship foundered as a result of words that were said or simply because of those that were not said? Pondering this state of affairs, it seemed to me better to risk forfeiting the relationship by telling her the truth than by slowly and painfully withdrawing from it out of what amounted to little more than abject cowardice. I knew that she had had a close friend, several years earlier, who was gay. I did not think she had forsaken him. Maybe, just maybe, she wouldn't abandon us as well.

Finally the inevitable Monday afternoon came when I was faced with a situation, similar to the one at choir rehearsal, that I simply could not ignore. I had to respond or risk losing totally my own self-respect as well as a close and trusted friend.

Nancy's youngest son had been to Kings Island, an amusement park over in Cincinnati, Ohio, the previous weekend. As it happened, that Saturday had been Gay Pride Day and the park itself had joined in the celebration by making a special invitation to the members of the lesbigay community. All gay men, lesbians and their friends and families were to wear red shirts as a sign of solidarity and in order to receive a special discount on the rides and attractions. The park was a virtual sea of crimson. Just by chance, Nancy's son was also wearing a red shirt that day. "Why, he said he would have beaten any of those queers to a bloody pulp, if they'd so much as laid a finger on him," Nancy recounted to me with proud disdain as we sipped our coffee. I knew the moment had arrived when I had to speak up. I decided it would be better not to blurt anything out in a rush, like some sort of desperate confession, but rather to simply narrate to her the story of how life at the Murray house had been over the last several weeks.

Her eyes grew wide and I could see that at times she was on the verge of tears. "Oh, Rhea!" she exclaimed, when I had finished. "I feel so ashamed that you went through all of this alone because you were afraid to tell me. And I know now just why you were so frightened. Please forgive all those thoughtless remarks. I didn't know how much I was hurting you. But you mustn't doubt my friendship, ever. Bruce is my heart's own child. That will never change. You must believe me."

My love for Nancy taught me to be patient and wait for her to grow in knowledge and understanding of the gay condition. Sometimes she would still make thoughtless remarks that were unintentionally hurtful. Once, for example, she told me she simply wouldn't be able to handle it if her boys turned out to be gay. In the beginning Nancy related to Bruce as though he had simply been afflicted with some disease, a horrible sickness that he couldn't help, as though he should be pitied. I tried gently to correct her on such points and found her to be generally receptive to alternative views. Secretly, she attended PFLAG meetings with my family to demonstrate her support. (She felt she had to be covert about going to PFLAG because of her husband's reaction.) Ironically, Nancy found as much support for herself at those first meetings as she was trying to demonstrate to us by going along.

I remember one early meeting where she was scolded rather vigorously by a young man for expressing her opinion that having a gay child would be like having a child that was severely handicapped or afflicted with some incurable disease. I could almost see the light bulb coming on over Nancy's head as she began to realize, from the young fellow's impassioned remarks, how terrible such opinions make gay people feel about themselves and that it's not pity gays and lesbians are after but rather the acceptance that comes through real human understanding. One of the qualities I have always loved and admired about my dear friend Nancy is her ability to admit it when she is wrong. It is a rare and valuable human characteristic indeed.

A year after that PFLAG meeting, we had both befriended a young man named Eddie, who was slowly dying of AIDS. Nancy had taken him straight to her heart and she was outraged by the insensitivity and rejection that he received, not only from the community, but from his own family.

For exercise, Nancy and I would often take brisk, six-a.m. walks in a local cemetery. (Somehow the sight of all those gravestones provides the perfect incentive to walk off some excess poundage.) I remember discussing Eddie's situation with her during one of our early-morning perambulations. Now, Nancy is a good six inches shorter than I am, but her anger at the way Eddie had been treated by his family got her totally riled. Soon she was walking so rapidly I had trouble keeping up. All the while, arms flailing in the air, she raged on about how they had no right to isolate him and how much their behavior increased his already unbearable suffering. With every word her pace seemed to accelerate. I was witnessing the birth of an activist before my very eyes and, though I was breathless from exhaustion when we finally stopped to rest, I had to smile.

Nancy owns a local beauty parlor. In recent months she has taken to wearing a big, easy-to-read button that says "Straight But Not Narrow" when she's in the shop. She has no compunction whatsoever about taking on a customer who happens to make a snide remark within her earshot about gay people. She will not tolerate it and she tells them so. If they don't like it, well, there's the front door. As a result she has lost some business. Amazingly, however, the lost customers have been made up through new ones who have heard about Nancy's stand on gay issues and happen to agree with her.

Despite considerable opposition from her family, she remains one of my staunchest allies. We have nurtured the hope in each other that surely if she and I could overcome our strictly bigoted, homophobic upbringing, then others of similar backgrounds can as well.

*

* *

My daughter's life was in turmoil. The father of her baby had agreed to marry her, but only as the result of pressure from his family to do so. He did not spare Tanya any of the effects of his intense unhappiness at having his young life saddled with the responsibilities of caring for a wife and child.

When we first learned of Bruce's homosexuality, Tanya was still pregnant. Butch and I decided it would be better to wait until after she had delivered her baby to break the news. Bruce himself was adamant that we not tell his sister, but that he be allowed to do it in his own way and when he felt the time was right. He greatly feared her reaction, and he did not wish to place his parents in the middle, caught, as it were, between their children.

As things turned out, unfortunately, Bruce's misgivings concerning Tanya's reaction were quite well founded. Suddenly, she became the archetypical homophobe, to the point of grotesque caricature. She began loudly to declaim "queer" jokes at every possible opportunity, especially when Bruce was present. Words like faggot, fruit, queer and fairy entered her vocabulary and she would go out of her way to employ them whenever she had the chance. Her desire to inflict as much pain as possible could hardly have been more blatantly obvious. Repeatedly, I asked her please to throttle these outrageous displays of bigotry, but to no avail. In fact, the more Butch and I protested, the nastier and more mean-spirited she became. It was hard to believe that this was the same girl who had saved up her allowance to buy her brother a special t-shirt as a gift when she was nine years old and he was but four.

Tanya and Bruce have always been very different. She is rather small and darkly beautiful, with huge brown eyes and black hair. Her perfect, white teeth give her a brilliantly winning smile that has always been difficult to say no to. She was rough-and-tumble, agile and a natural athlete. She could roller-skate, ice-skate and water-ski well, all on the very first try.

Bruce, on the other hand, is tall, green-eyed and fair complexioned. He is not in the least athletic (though the continued harassment and threats of physical violence from school-yard bullies and street punks eventually did lead to his learning martial-arts techniques purely for the sake of self-preservation). As a child, in fact, he was even a little awkward, but he has since grown out of it. He loves nature and being out-of-doors, but his temperament and sensibilities are of a gentler sort. He is thoughtful, and leans more toward the artistic and creative than his sister ever did.

They have both always made friends easily. But where Bruce knocked himself out to please others, Tanya's aim was to persuade others to please her.

I believe Bruce was trying to protect me by not wanting to tell Tanya of his homosexuality in the beginning. When Tanya feels vulnerable or afraid her reaction is to go on the attack, to lash out. More often than not, I was the focus of her rages. It was a pattern that had developed from her misplaced anger over her adoption. Bruce knew his sister well and wanted to be sure I was prepared for the consequences of revealing to her that her baby brother was a homosexual.

In all fairness, it must be said that Tanya had been through a lot just prior to learning that Bruce was gay. Besides her untimely pregnancy and finding herself trapped in a marriage that neither she nor her husband wanted, she had also recently had a rather shockingly unpleasant reunion with her birth mother.

It soon became clear, however, that her anger did not spring from any real personal abhorrence for Bruce. Rather, it arose out of fear. I remember one poignant moment when she declared that she couldn't stand to talk about her brother's homosexuality because she didn't like the thought of having to bury him when he died of AIDS. Though her words were like daggers to me, they did indicate her reaction was motivated by sheer dread and panic rather than out of some form of hatred. As time passed, where there had been angry outbursts, there now arose a wall of stony silence.

Until one evening, several months later, when we were all sitting in the backyard reminiscing about the family vacations we all used to take together. We would sometimes assume different names while traveling so we could be as outrageous as we wanted while claiming to be someone else. Once we became the Harvey Smith family from Walla Walla, Washington. I was Mary Sue Beth, Tanya was Magpie, and Bruce: Billy Joe Bob. We had a lot of good laughs remembering some of the hilarious incidents that befell the Harvey Smiths on their travels. Suddenly, in the midst of our happy chatter, Tanya fell silent.

"I don't feel like I've been a very good sister to you," she said, turning to Bruce, tears welling in her eyes. "I haven't been there for you when you really needed me."

"Aw, I've always known you loved me, sis," Bruce replied, taking her gently into his arms. "Remember how you used to play hot wheels with me all the time when we were little? I knew you weren't that crazy about hot wheels. You did it because you loved me. And remember that t-shirt you bought for me with your allowance? — Or, how about the time when I was five and you convinced me to snort some pepper up my nose in front of our friends? I thought I'd never stop sneezing," he laughed.

"Yeah," Tanya chimed in, drying her eyes. "I remember the way you covered for me when mom came in wanting to know what was going on. You said you thought it was an attack of allergies. Man, Bruce, I thought I'd killed you."

With that, everyone broke into renewed laughter born of the joyous realization that we were still a family after all, bonded each one to the others by our rich trove of wonderful, loving memories.

CHAPTER

IX

My family sincerely wanted to accept pastor Robert's apology. If loving compassion is truly at the heart of the gospel of Christ, how could we proclaim that gospel and withhold our forgiveness? So, we decided the best thing to do was to try to continue attending church as before, just as though nothing had happened.

But the former joy I had taken in church activities, such as Wednesday evening choir rehearsal, eluded me now. It had been replaced by a vague and awkward sense of uneasiness and estrangement. Try as I might to recapture the old feeling of pure delight, in my heart I knew it was gone for good. Though the people were all the same ones I had known and loved for such a long time, and nothing about the physical surroundings of the place had changed, I still felt distinctly like an outsider. It was a feeling I simply could not seem to shake off.

The music did continue to be a source of great pleasure, however. We were getting ready for Easter, and I was thrilled at the prospect of singing Handel's "Hallelujah Chorus" for the Easter Sunday service. One of my fondest wishes had always been to be a member of a choir that was singing this glorious work. I smiled inwardly as I came to the realization that providing me the opportunity of performing in this piece of music would probably be the church's farewell gift to me.

The piece was a challenge for our little choir, and more than once the director considered replacing it with something a little more within our capabilities. We were rehearsing right down to the last few minutes before the service. Even Rev. Roberts appeared to doubt our ability to carry it off.

Finally the moment arrived. The organist played the short introduction and an instant later the choir jumped in for all we were worth. I sang as if my life depended upon it. I sang for all my many lost illusions about my church and for the friends I had once believed I had there but whose love, when put to the test, had failed me. It was my swan song. I could feel the hair on the back of my neck standing on end. I couldn't believe my ears! We sounded so majestic, and the volume seemed that of a chorus three times our size. It was beautiful. When the final chord sounded, we were all breathless. A pin could have been heard falling on plush carpet, so still was it. Then suddenly someone in the congregation began to clap, then another and another till the entire church was filled with grateful applause (which goes very much against the rather stuffy protocols of traditional Presbyterian worship). The minister turned and regarded us with pure amazement. He shared with the congregation his earlier misgivings concerning our ability to do justice to Mr. Handel's music and declared that an Easter miracle had surely taken place. "Beautiful, choir!" he exclaimed. "Absolutely beautiful!" I smiled and whispered a prayer of thanksgiving.

But the elation of that moment could not halt the deterioration of our relationship with the church. One Sunday, perhaps two or three weeks later, I was standing with Bruce in the corridor outside the choir room. I was feeling depressed because the shunning of my son by the congregation had become so blatantly obvious. On that particular day he had been spoken to by literally no one, though he had greeted many in his usual friendly, outgoing manner. As he and I stood there together, preparing to leave for home, Linda, the choir director, came up to me and, with great concern in her eyes, gently touched my arm. "Are you all right, my dear?" she asked, completely ignoring Bruce, refusing even to acknowledge his presence with a glance or a smile.

"Was that look of pity she gave you because I'm your son?" he said with noticeable bitterness, after Linda had walked on down the hall.

It was at that moment I suddenly realized what was expected of me by the good people of Grace Presbyterian: I could personally reap all the benefits of their love and sympathy, and regain their meanly withheld fellowship if I would only allow myself to be viewed as the victim of my son's recalcitrant homosexuality. If I were willing, in other words, to sacrifice him upon the altar of their benighted prejudice, I could then be welcomed back into the fold with open, if pitying, arms. Another trip to Moriah was staring me dead in the face.

Sacrifice my son so you can love me? Not in this lifetime!

Clearly, our association with the church had reached a critical turning point. The price of acceptance there had become a bit too steep. My close, loving relationship with my son was simply not negotiable, and to continue to expect him to go on attending services only to endure the congregation's stony rejection was patently unkind and unfair to him, not to mention unreasonable. How could I enter the front door of that church if I was expected to leave my son, my own flesh and blood, standing outside alone, falsely maligned and rejected, on the sidewalk? Most Christians would probably give some degree of lip service to the notion that homosexuality is "unnatural," but to me it was plain as day that nothing on earth could be any more unnatural than a mother's abandoning her own child, whatever the reason.

After our first two weeks or so of absence from services, I received a card from a church member who wrote that she had missed seeing my face among the choir on Sunday mornings. I called to thank her for her kindness in sending me the note, but when she recognized my voice on the phone all she said was: "I know what this is all about, and I don't want any part of it." Whereupon she abruptly hung up on me. I was stunned. Why had she sent me the card, then? I felt almost as though I'd been set up. After a little reflection, however, it became obvious to me that this woman (along with most of the rest of the congregation) was deeply conflicted, caught between her affection for me and her intractable persistence in the stereotypical views she clung to concerning Bruce's homosexuality. My insistence on not only accepting but openly supporting my son apparently presented this woman, as well as the church as a whole, with a totally unreconcilable dilemma.

And so Bruce, Butch and I stayed away, even though doing so felt like a piece of our lives had been torn from us. All other options appeared to have been exhausted. It was like being confronted with a stone wall a thousand miles long and ten miles high. Taking Rev. Roberts at his word, we came quite honestly to believe that no church would ever accept us. Just a short distance outside Sunnyside, the Indiana State Wildlife Refuge at Muscatatuck became our sanctuary. It was for us a source of renewal and communion with God through nature. Many, many Sundays were spent there, during that long, sad summer of 1993. PFLAG also greatly helped to fill the void. Its members served as priests, confessors and comforters to us and shining examples of what loving fellowship ought to be. Rev. Roberts never contacted us to find out why we had stopped attending his church nor to encourage us to return.

*

*   *

We did go back one more time, however. That first Christmas as outsiders was particularly difficult. With each passing Sunday in the Advent season the memory of our church's friendly, festive yuletide atmosphere grew stronger. Our hearts ached for the loss of our Christian community. Christmas at the Murray house that year had more the feeling of a wake than a joyous and merry celebration. At last we broke down, deciding we simply couldn't get through the holiday without attending church at least once.

The candle-light service on Christmas Eve had been the emotional apex of the liturgical year for us. We looked forward to it with mounting anticipation from Thanksgiving onward. In my memory of Christmases long gone by I still can picture the sanctuary bathed in warm, soft light when we entered, in splendid contrast to the cold, shadowy street outside. A throng of friendly, welcoming faces would greet us as we took our seats, mine in the choir loft, and Butch and Bruce in one of the pews up front. An air of festive celebration flooded to every corner of the spacious, high-ceilinged auditorium.

Christmas Eve 1993 was very different, however. Bruce, Butch and I all commented to each other later that entering the sanctuary that night was more like walking into a cold, dusky cave than the warm and welcoming environment of our memories. Many just stared at us in disbelief and icy silence, but few would allow their eyes to meet our gaze. After the service, several people did approach us. A few choir members hugged us and offered words of kindness even to Bruce. Some tears were shed. Linda, the choir director was particularly affectionate toward Bruce, which surprised me greatly, given her former attitude.

The entire experience was altogether bewildering to me. What did this sudden rush of attention on the part of several church members on Christmas Eve mean, after so long a time of silent neglect? Was it just some temporary manifestation of "holiday spirit," or was there anything more substantial and lasting to it? In an attempt to resolve the situation in my own mind, a few days later I tried to put my feelings into words by writing a letter to Linda. I told her how good it was to see all my old choir buddies on Christmas Eve, but that I didn't know if a door was opening up for my family and me at the church, or if this was its final closing. I said I knew that no one had set out deliberately to hurt me at that fateful choir rehearsal, now nearly a year ago. I know these people, I said. They are not the type to deliberately inflict pain and suffering. I'm sure for them the talk about gay people that night was just another lively discussion. But for me it hit home in a personal way because they were talking about my child. The fact that they didn't know Bruce was gay at the time made little difference because a person who categorically vilifies homosexuals may never know if a gay or lesbian person, their parents, siblings or friends might be standing right next to them hearing, and feeling, every hateful word.

I know my son is a good and moral person, I wrote. He did not choose to be gay. Of this I am certain. What man or woman would choose to be so hated and reviled just for being who they are? I told her how verbal and physical abuse against my son had escalated dramatically since Rev. Roberts speculated publicly concerning Bruce's homosexuality. I said I greatly feared for his safety, even for his life.

I told Linda that I knew the choir members were sorry for having hurt me personally, but I did not feel they were sorry for their prejudice and it is the prejudice that has the power to wound more deeply than anything. I reminded her of how she had shunned Bruce in my presence that day in the corridor outside the choir room, and how the experience had made me realize I would have to sacrifice my son if I wanted to be received back into the fellowship of the church. But my heart would never allow me to abandon my child, I explained.

I ended this letter asking Linda if she believed my family's relationship with the church could be restored and whether the embraces we had received from choir members on Christmas Eve were hugs of acceptance or hugs of farewell. Sadly, her response was no response. I never heard from her directly concerning my letter, though another choir member later confided to me that Linda had not responded because she didn't feel she could "win." How strange, I thought, as though one's struggle for understanding could be reduced to some childish game that had to be won or lost.

Several months later I was contacted by a member of Grace Presbyterian, who asked me to participate in an interdenominational women's Bible study group. It had been my experience in the past that such groups often involved intense, intimate sharing. I informed the woman that if I was going to take part in these discussions I should not be expected to censor my life. "There is much we need to learn," she said, "and who better to teach us?" This statement gave me a glimmer of hope.

At the third meeting of the study group one of the women, a doctor's wife, asked me why I was wearing a red AIDS ribbon on my blouse. I explained that I had been a proctor for the AIDS Memorial Quilt when it had come to Bloomington the previous weekend. She sneered at this, screwing up her face in disgust and saying: "It is difficult to feel sorry for those people, considering what they did to get it."

I explained calmly that in Africa AIDS has been spread almost altogether through heterosexual intercourse. There, the vast majority of its victims are straight people. I told her the reason AIDS had spread so rapidly through the gay community in the United States was probably only because it was first introduced and gained a foothold in that sector of the population. She seemed unimpressed until I told her she should have seen the vast number of quilt panels for little babies.

"Babies get AIDS?" she asked with lingering incredulity, but melting a little. (This struck me as particularly odd, coming, as it did, from the wife of a medical practitioner.)

"There was also a panel for a mother of six. It read 'I can't be finished, I'm not done yet.' Besides," I observed quietly, "they're all somebody's baby."

I told her that I was the mother of a gay son. Her main concern upon learning this was how I could reconcile Holy

Scripture with Bruce's homosexuality without disowning him. The choice seemed perfectly clear to her. Then, abruptly changing the subject, she asked me if there was homosexual behavior among the animal kingdom. Now I could add animals to the growing list of subhuman creatures to which Bruce had been compared, a list that included murderers, drug addicts, alcoholics, child molesters and rapists. During this entire discussion the others in the group sat silently, many with downcast eyes.

One member of the study group was from mainland China. She was married to an American and had not been long in the United States. Her name was Kai. She usually rode with me to the meetings. I liked Kai and her quiet, gentle ways, but I was never sure how much she understood since her English was still quite tentative and faltering. I had read that the Chinese do not even have a word for homosexuality in their language. That afternoon, following the discussion with the doctor's wife, I was very depressed during the drive home. Kai sat in the front seat next to me, and I was fighting to hide my emotions from her, not knowing how much she would be able to understand. Suddenly she reached over and seized my right hand.

"It be all right. You see," she said, in her halting English.

"Thank you, Kai" I replied, a little astonished.

"Your son, he be all right too."

"Thank you."

"Your son, he be all right too!" she reiterated. "You see. You . . . you try too hard."

"Oh?"

"Yes, your son, he be all right!" she repeated emphatically. "Once I lived by two lesbian. They love each other very much. Had good life. Your son, he have good life too. He find somebody to love. He have good life too. You see. Don't try so hard! You only playing piano for cows."

I burst out laughing. Playing piano for cows was indeed a perfect metaphor, and the laughter it inspired rescued me from another plunge into despair.

CHAPTER X

By the late fall of 1993, the situation at the high school had become highly volatile. Each day presented Bruce with a fresh ordeal to endure. It became so dangerous for him to go to the isolated side corridor where his locker was located that he took to dragging all his books around with him rather than visit the locker to drop off and pick up what he needed. The mere task of making it from one classroom to the next required a herculean effort. He was often tripped, slammed against lockers, punched and kicked. His text and note books would be knocked from his arms, loose-leaf pages flying in all directions. Such episodes often caused him to be slightly late for class, whereupon the teacher would frequently launch into a diatribe concerning Bruce's tardiness, thus further humiliating him before his peers.

There was not a lot of support or sympathy among the teachers for Bruce's predicament. On the contrary, teachers were often openly hostile toward him, making little, if any, effort to conceal their utter disdain. The general consensus, among the faculty and administration, seems to have been that he had brought all this abuse upon himself. After all, he could change if he wanted to. One day a fellow student stabbed Bruce in the buttocks with a stiletto-sharp pencil. This attack took place in full view of a teacher who, when Bruce cried out in pain, sneered: "I thought you would've probably enjoyed that."

Of course, there were some few exceptions who considered Bruce's treatment to be utterly ghastly and sometimes even said so. They would draw him aside and offer words of encouragement, telling him to "just hang in there," or "keep your chin up." Once, a teacher even went so far as to take some of her male colleagues to task for their mocking and taunting of my son. Her protests only succeeded in bringing down the scornful wrath of these crude vulgarians on her own head. From then on she found herself nearly as ostracized as Bruce was. At the end of the term, in complete disgust, she resigned to seek employment elsewhere, an option, unfortunately, unavailable to my son.

Filthy remarks were constantly hurled at Bruce by his fellow students. He could be simply walking down the hall from one class to the next when some passing stranger would shout: "Hey, Murray, suck my dick." or "There goes Murray, the faggot cocksucker." The school has a so-called anti-sexual-harassment policy. It prescribes automatic expulsion for offenders. In Bruce's case, however, this policy was never once enforced against his persecutors.

One of Bruce's few friends, Steve, was a frail youth from a family of Jehovah's Witnesses. He was tortured by his homosexuality and the direct conflict it placed him in with his family's staunch religious beliefs. Even uttering the word "homosexual" in his mother's presence had earned Steve a slap across the face. Bruce was aware of his friend's desperate situation and his fragile emotional state. He was worried that Steve might act upon an impulse to commit suicide, an option with which Bruce himself was all too familiar.

In art class, the two friends sat near the front of the room in the hope that by being within the teacher's hearing range they might escape some of the relentless harassment. It was a futile effort. The boys were seated directly in front of the teacher's desk one day when suddenly someone, from the back of the class, yelled: "Hey, Steve, are you a perverted sperm sucker too?" But the teacher, obviously pretending not to have heard, didn't even raise his head.

Bruce had had enough. He jumped to his feet. "I can't believe you're not going to do anything about that," he said to the teacher.

"About what?" the art instructor replied with a smirk on his face.

"I know you heard that," Bruce declared. "The entire class heard it."

"Heard what?"

"If you refuse to do anything about this," Bruce stated, in disbelief, "then I want to speak to my counselor."

"I won't give you a pass," the teacher stated flatly

"Then I'll take care of it on my own time," my son replied. "But you can be sure that I will do something about this."

Rather than go to the weak, passive man who was his regular counselor, Bruce decided to take the problem to a female counselor who was known to have a bit more gumption. Action was indeed forthcoming. The counselor monitored the class for several days thereafter. This accomplished little, however, except to cause the teacher some degree of embarrassment. Of course, everyone was on their best behavior while the counselor was in the room. But as soon as the monitoring was discontinued the instructor moved the boys to the very back of the room. Immediately, the harassment resumed and from that point on both Steve and Bruce, who had both always gotten above average marks in art, received nothing but failing grades on every assignment they turned in.

I went frequently to the school to try to rectify the situation. I asked for conferences with the parents of the offending students, but was refused even my request for their names. Often the harassers were total strangers to Bruce. At each of these visits, Mr. Fielding, Bruce's male counselor, would assure me that he would take care of everything, but none of the offenders ever received more than the mildest of reprimands. Later, they would even use the fact that they were not punished as another way of taunting Bruce.

Eventually, at my son's request, I stopped going. "Mom, I want to fight my own battles," he told me. "I have to show them I can stand on my own two feet." It made me feel quite inadequate to just stand idly by, but my trips to the school did absolutely no good, and I sensed that they might even be making matters worse.

Then Bruce began taking martial arts training. He would practice by sparring with his dad in the back yard, and, as one student soon discovered, became quite adept at blocking punches and delivering retribution.

As was often the case, Bruce was simply walking down the hall on his way to class when he suddenly found himself surrounded by a group of several boys. "Hey, Bruce, you fucking faggot!" one of them shouted and shoved him up against the wall. Another started to administer a blow. In one swift, smooth move, Bruce countered the punch, catching the boy's arm and twisting it painfully behind his back. The young man cried out in distress. "Just remember it was a faggot that nailed your ass," Bruce said, before turning the boy loose and letting him drop to the floor in agony. As he walked away, he heard the other boys chiding their humiliated friend for having been bested by a "fairy."

One afternoon I received a phone call from the principal's office asking me to come to the school and pick Bruce up. He was having an asthma attack and had collapsed in gym class while running laps.

"But why on earth were you running?" I asked my ashen-faced, wheezing son, as we drove home. "You have a doctor's statement on file saying that you should never be permitted to run in gym class."

"I told the gym teacher, mom, but he said I would have to take gym over if I didn't run. I'd rather die than go through another year of gym," he said, the sound of desperate humiliation in his voice. "The locker room is unbearable. Mom, they spit on me."

Such deliberate acts of humiliation as spitting on another person took my breath away. The mistreatment that Bruce was being subjected to, at the hands of teachers as well as his peers, far surpassed any abuse I had experienced as a child. These were assaults of a darker, far more sinister nature than anything I had witnessed in my life. These were attacks upon Bruce's dignity, his humanity, motivated by nothing but senseless, wanton hatred. I felt I could have borne the pain myself. It was being forced to helplessly watch my son's agony that was too much to suffer. To me it was worse than the severest beating I had ever received at the hands of my father or my first husband. I had never experienced such bitterness as now began to rage inside me.

Finally the inevitable breaking point was reached. Bruce arrived home from school one sunny, spring afternoon with a dark bruise on his chin. He was very distressed and agitated over an encounter he had had that day with Matt, an African-American student, who took particular delight in tormenting him.

Matt was a star athlete. He enjoyed sports greatly, but his favorite game was what was known around Sunnyside High as "smear the queer." Matthew had been reported innumerable times for harassing Bruce, both verbally and physically. As usual, however, no meaningful disciplinary action was ever taken against him.

On the day in question, Matt had once again attacked Bruce in the hall, calling him a faggot and slamming him up against a bank of lockers. This time, however, Bruce's control snapped. "Leave me the hell alone, you nigger!" he screamed.

Matt responded immediately with a sharp punch to Bruce's jaw. Bruce countered the blow with a swift, martial-arts kick to Matthew's midsection sending him to the floor, doubled up in pain.

I pulled the story out of my son in bits and pieces. Before he had finished telling me the whole thing, however, he was sobbing uncontrollably. Crying, not because he had lost control, not because he had injured Matt, not even because of his own relentless humiliation. It was because he had applied the word "nigger" to another human being that he wept such bitter tears.

"Oh, mom! Oh, mom!" he cried. "I'm so ashamed. Look what this is turning me into! There's this rage that just keeps building and building inside me and look what it's doing to me! I'm becoming like them! I'm becoming like people who use words like nigger and faggot and kike and . . . and God knows what. And there's real hatred there, mom, I mean real hatred!" He looked almost maniacal. It sent a tremor of fear through my body. "I don't know what I might do the next time. I'm afraid, mom. I'm afraid of what I might do . . . of what I might do to them."

Now, there was no doubt in my mind that Bruce would not spend another year at Sunnyside High School. I had come to understand all too well the rage of which my son had spoken. It kept my husband and me awake many a night. It robbed our lives of all joy and meaning and supplanted them with anger and pain. The darkness of hatred was gaining a foothold within my family. It was shaping us into the likeness of our enemies. It had to be stopped. No matter what steps must be taken, I was going to get Bruce out of that loathsome, hostile environment that passed itself off as a place of learning. There were only two weeks left in the term, so I would have the entire summer to plan my strategy.

On the last day of school, in the spring of 1994, Bruce was informed that he must pay for damage to his locker, despite the fact that he had not even used it since the first few weeks of classes. Apparently, this locker had received near constant vandalism throughout the year. When school officials opened it, they could not believe their eyes (or noses). The locker was filled with trash, garbage and rotting food. It seems that some of the students of Sunnyside High had used the locker as a trash receptacle. It had become an eloquent symbol, a monument to their utter contempt for a queer boy in their midst. Bruce did manage to convince officials that he was not responsible for the damage to his locker, and the fee was finally waived.

Later that same afternoon, Bruce and Steve were standing on the sidewalk outside the school. As Steve stepped from the curb into the street, Bruce heard a pick-up truck, just a few feet away, rev its engine ominously. Instinctively, he grabbed Steve's arm and pulled him back onto the sidewalk as the vehicle sped past, just inches from the curb. Of course the word "faggot" was screamed from the truck as it roared away. Steve and Bruce looked at each other in stunned but knowing silence. Death hovered close by that day.

*
*   *

As soon as the summer vacation started, I began to notice the change in Bruce. Tension would drain away from his face and shoulders. His smile returned and laughter once again rang out in the Murray house. Since childhood, our son has had a delightful sense of humor. He was so different now from the dark, sullen boy he had been but a week or two earlier. The change only deepened my resolve to free him from the oppressive school environment.

Moving was not an option. Butch had too many years in at Cummins Engine to sacrifice his retirement. Also, my daughter's life was still in crisis. I couldn't abandon her. Home tutoring or correspondence school were beginning to look like our only options. After weeks of research, I settled on a correspondence school out of Chicago. It was over a hundred years old, had a good reputation and was accredited by the North Central Conference. Furthermore, it was within our budget. I sent off for information and an application.

The first step was the hardest. Before I could enroll Bruce with the correspondence school, I would have to secure a release from the school in Sunnyside. I called Bruce's counselor, Mr. Fielding, and explained to him about the release. "Oh, Mrs. Murray," he said. "Our principal, Mr. McDill, will never sign your release. He is totally against home schooling. I would be very surprised if you can get him to agree to it."

My heart sank. Suppose McDill gave me a hard time. Suppose he refused to sign the release. Bruce was counting on me, and the summer was already beginning to wane. Quickly, I formulated a plan. I picked up the phone and made an appointment to see McDill the very next day.

A flood of memories washed over me the following afternoon, as I entered the high school where many years earlier I too had been a student. Walking into McDill's office, I felt like an ill-behaved child who had been sent to the principal for disciplining. I fought back those memories and feelings along with my dread of male authority figures (a remnant from another part of my childhood, no doubt). Nothing must be allowed to stand in the way of my facing Mr. McDill as an equal. The principal entered his office and shook my cold, trembling hand. My smile belied the butterflies fluttering around in my belly.

"Now, what can I do for you today, Mrs. Murray?" he asked.

"I have some release papers here for you to sign so my son, Bruce, can be enrolled in a correspondence school."

He scowled. "Now, why ever would you want to remove your son from our school system?"

"Because he is not safe here," I replied. "And you seem unable to protect him."

"So, you feel your son has been singled out for abuse. Is that it?"

"Yes, I do."

"And just why is that, Mrs. Murray?" he asked, his tone at once unctuous and interrogating.

Leaning forward, I caught the man's eyes and held them with my own. *Don't you dare to look away from me,*

I thought. "It's because my son is gay," I said flatly, pronouncing each word with clear distinction. I held his gaze a moment longer, in the brief, tense silence that followed. My straightforwardness had startled him. He appeared a bit uneasy now, not quite so in command of the situation as he had been but a few seconds earlier. I knew then that I was initiating Mr. McDill into a brand new experience: A parent, and a woman, no less, announcing forcefully and totally without shame that her son was gay. In that moment the ground shifted beneath my feet. Mr. McDill and I were now on equal territory.

"Sir," I continued, breaking the silence. "My son will not endure another school year like the last. The way I see it, there are only two options: You will either sign this release so he can take correspondence courses, or I will contact the Indiana Civil Liberties Union, and any other group I can think of, to bring as much pressure as possible to bear on you and this school." Wordlessly, McDill shifted in his chair. "Bruce is only fifteen years old," I said. "I would hate to see him outed any more publicly than he has already been by some in this community who consider themselves quite honorable and responsible citizens. But you can be certain, sir, that if my son has to suffer, as he has had to in the past, I'm going to see to it that you and this school take some heat for it. — So, Mr. McDill, will you sign these forms, or do you, Bruce and I spend the next year on the front page of every newspaper in the country?"

Without speaking, the principal reached across the desk, picked up the forms and scrawled his signature on them. As I turned to leave, my son's freshly signed release from hell clutched tightly in my fist, McDill took his parting shot. "Unfortunately, Mrs. Murray, many doors are going to be closed to your son," he said.

I did not respond to the principal's extremely conventional remark, but made up my mind then and there that none of life's opportunities were going to be denied my son simply because he was gay. What right did this man, this bureaucrat, or anyone else for that matter, have to place such limitations on Bruce's future? The world teems with possibilities, and Sunnyside definitely was not representative of that world. Together, my son and I would explore the real world, the one whose boundaries are set only by the limits of a person's vision, abilities and determination. I left McDill's office that day with a new sense of pride and freedom, as though life, with all its infinite scope, were beginning afresh.

There were moments, over the ensuing two years, when I had grave doubts as to whether I had chosen the right course. Many have felt called upon to volunteer their unsolicited opinions concerning my decision to remove Bruce from the public school system. They felt I should have fought back and held the system accountable. I can truly see the validity of their position. At the time, however, I was more concerned with the safety, well-being and, indeed, survival of my child, than I was about taking a public stand on an issue of social justice. I didn't feel I could take the risk of placing Bruce back in Sunnyside High School while I battled away at the system in the courts and public media, doubtlessly stirring up intense controversy and increased rancor in an already hostile community. It was more important for our son to survive and get an education than it was for him to become some cause célèbre or an engine for social change. Even now, I know in my heart that I am still a mother before I'm an activist.

Then, of course, there were the nagging insecurities over my taking on the full responsibility for Bruce's education. I had been out of school for twenty-five years. Now, here I was facing algebra, geometry and French! Had I bitten off more than I could chew? Many nights I sat up trying to conquer a stubborn algebra or geometry equation in preparation for Bruce's lessons the following day. I would go to bed only to jump up a few minutes later, much to my husband's dismay, rush back to the dining room table and tackle the problem anew.

Butch was wonderful. He pitched in with the house-work and even the cooking, as my time became more and more consumed with Bruce's studies. My husband would smile and shake his head in admiration as he watched his wife and son struggle with some daunting problem, a pile of crumpled papers at their feet.

We took field trips to museums, factories, and the theater. Bruce and I saw our first Broadway musical together. We were on a mission of exploration and discovery, and it became clear that my world was beginning to expand as much as his.

Together we discovered our mutual fondness for the musical plays of Andrew Lloyd Weber. I was deeply touched recently when my son presented me with a recording of collected songs from Weber's shows. "Mom, I want you to know that I realize what a sacrifice you've made by teaching me at home," he said. "I know you haven't had much time for your piano or your painting. I don't think I ever really knew how much you love me until now."

Sacrifice?! All this extra time spent with my son expanding our understanding of the world, ourselves and each other was a wonderful gift. It's hard for me to find the sacrifice in that.

CHAPTER XI

The world was beginning to unfold for me now in new ways with each passing day. After such a long period of tremendous loss and increasing isolation, my life was finally entering a new phase of growth and adventure, with a continuous stream of fascinating new people and situations arriving on the scene seemingly every other moment. Life was teeming with newly discovered diversity and possibility, and the realization of it suddenly made me see, perhaps for the very first time, how utterly parochial and insular my Sunnyside existence had been. I was meeting more interesting people in a matter of months than I had met in my entire life, and each new man or woman was a source of greater knowledge and understanding, not only of that person but of the larger world, outside my narrow experience, which they represented. Because my coming to terms with my son's gayness had given me the precious gift of empathy, I was influenced, sometimes quite profoundly, by the life experience of each new human being I came to know. My everyday life became like a classroom where I was presented with an endless procession of living, breathing lessons in humanity.

The activities of my family continued to be largely centered around our PFLAG meetings. One particular Wednesday evening our Bloomington group had gathered at the home of one of its members. It turned out to be a very emotional meeting, as there were many new participants that night, and the first few meetings are usually the most difficult for newcomers. At some point during the evening someone mentioned to me that we were no longer the only folks from Sunnyside in the chapter, and pointed out a shy young man.

Within a matter of minutes after meeting him, Michael had won my heart and was well on his way to becoming an integral part of my family. He shared with me the now all-too-familiar story of acknowledging to himself that he was gay and how it had driven him to the very brink of suicide. His journey had been complicated, yet again, by inflexible religious beliefs. Michael came from a family of devout Jehovah's Witnesses. He knew that by coming out publicly he would not only be "disfellowshipped" (roughly analogous to being excommunicated) by the congregation, but banished from his family as well, who would no longer even allow themselves to recognize his presence among them. Such acts of sheer familial abandonment, especially by mothers and fathers, never fail to astound and perplex me even today, after having seen so many such tragic cases.

From that evening on, Michael became a child of my heart. He spent many hours with my family as its new and celebrated member, gracing our lives with his quiet kindnesses and gentle insights. His musical ability has brought all of us many happy hours of joyful entertainment. Michael is such a warm and giving person, and we are better people because he is a part of our lives. It is indeed a very real tragedy that his parents, out of little more than implacable ignorance, would choose to cut themselves off from the great pleasure that comes with taking true delight in one's children. We eagerly accepted Michael as a wondrous gift to our lives, a gift that his blood family had so callously, and foolishly, cast aside.

How does such rejection of one's own offspring represent anything like the so-called "family values" we hear so much about? My experience with Michael caused me to reëxamine my concept of what a family actually is. The conclusion that I have come to is that a family can be any unit of people coming together to embrace, support and accept one another in an environment of mutual respect, trust, and unconditional love with a spirit of celebration.

Close on the heels of meeting Michael came a second PFLAG encounter with people from Sunnyside. The moment Dwight and Caroline entered the room we recognized each other. For an instant fear and apprehension crossed their faces, but after our first few minutes of conversation they were visibly more relaxed. Their son had come out to them some five years earlier. I considered it a little unusual that their struggle still seemed so intense, their pain still fresh after such a long time, but I just assumed they had become somehow stuck along the way on their journey toward acceptance and were now seeking to move forward once again. I was overjoyed to meet others from my town who were traveling the same road as I was. We began spending a lot of time together, as gradually Dwight and Caroline's long, bitter struggle began to unfold.

After their son had come out to them, Dwight had descended into a dark, all-engulfing depression. One evening, in a state of hopeless despair and bitter frustration, he confessed to his wife of thirty years that he too was in fact gay. Suddenly many troubling and mysterious pieces of their life together began to fall devastatingly into place. Dwight's long periods of dark moodiness, that he could never quite explain, and for which his wife and children had always felt somehow vaguely responsible, took on new significance. Gradually, as my husband and I looked on, the fabric of these good people's life together began to unravel. We bore witness to their struggles, tears, rages, agony and confusion as well as their love. We helped them to move into their separate homes, and into their now quite sad and singular lives. The vision of Caroline, crumpled in tears in the corner of the empty master bedroom of what had once been their dream house, will be forever etched in my memory. Both their lives were in ruins.

To me, the ordeal of Caroline and Dwight was a bitter lesson in one of our society's most insidiously evil injustices. Many thousands of young gay men and lesbians every year succumb to the overwhelming social pressure to conform to what is "expected" of them by entering into heterosexual marriages. These unions (if "union" is in fact the correct term here) are usually little more than cruel charades that, more often than not, end in tragic and resentful unhappiness for all concerned. Curiously, it seems that many parents would rather see their gay children trapped in marriages that make the kids' lives a living hell than have to deal openly, honestly and acceptingly with a son's or a daughter's homosexuality. Also, because the socialization process, even in childhood, consistently equates homosexuality with shame and disgrace, as young adults many gays and lesbians come to view heterosexual marriage as a means of escaping what they perceive as life-long pariah status. Or, if not an escape, at least marriage looks seductively (and deceptively) like a safe place in which to hide. The perpetuation of this process of repression does a cruel disservice to all our children, straight, gay and bisexual alike.

*

*   *

When I first met Eddie, there were still enough traces of his former self to tell me that he had once been a strikingly handsome man. We were introduced by a mutual friend when Eddie had come home from San Francisco to see his family. He had enormous sky-blue eyes that seemed to be magnified by his thin face and sunken cheeks. Those eyes had a frightened look about them, like a deer's when it is caught in the headlights of an on-coming car on a midnight's country road. His body was frail and thin, and he reminded me of a small bird with broken wings. He was a man in his mid thirties dying of AIDS.

There were things Eddie needed to tell his family before he died, and he had made the long, difficult journey from California to Indiana to say them. The family, however, met his invitation to have an honest exchange with a wall of silence as impenetrable as any made of stone. It was obvious that they loved Eddie, but he was being walled out of his family's life by the barrier of their own discomfort about AIDS and about the very fact of his being gay. They couldn't bridge the gap. They were too afraid of being discomforted by having to interrogate their own feelings.

In his sorrow and frustration, Eddie turned to me. He spent many hours pouring out his thoughts and feelings, sharing the priceless treasures of his innermost self with me, rather than with the biological family who needed most to hear, understand and celebrate his life. Eddie was obsessed with concern for his mother, whom he would soon be leaving behind, and for all the many things he feared would be left undone and unsaid. I often held him in my arms as he wept bitter tears born of the pain of frustration, rejection and abandonment.

When Eddie returned to San Francisco he told the circle of friends who had become his real family about his experiences with the nice lady from Sunnyside. They found it very difficult to believe there was *anyone* in the Midwest who was straight and could possibly have fit the open and affirming picture that Eddie painted of me. (Inaccurate stereotypes sometimes hinder trusting acceptance in the gay community too.) At last, dubbing me the "Fairy Princess," they decided to pool their resources and fly me out to California for a visit with Eddie. Conquering my fear of flying was one thing. Conquering my mother's staunch objections to my traveling two thousand miles only to have to rely on the kindness of strangers (like poor Blanche DuBois) when I arrived was another matter altogether. Finally mom relented, and I boarded a plane bound for San Francisco.

The rascal in me couldn't resist fashioning a homemade crown and scepter to wear for the arrival of the "princess" in her "fairyland." The men who greeted me at the airport howled with delighted surprise and appreciation at my campy shenanigans. They had a surprise or two of their own, however. First, I was presented with a huge bouquet of roses. Then, I was whisked away in a stretch limo to the heart of the city's Castro district where Eddie lived.

For the next eight days I became the surrogate mother to a large group of wonderful, loving young men. I found myself in the midst of an entire society of grown-up, gay orphans who were starving for the maternal care and affection that had long ago been withdrawn from them. In most instances rejection had come simply because they had needed to share the intimate truths of who they were with their mothers. To be sure, they gave their fairy princess the royal treatment, wining and dining and generally providing me with enough fun and excitement to last an entire lifetime. But they also shared with me their stories of pain, overwhelming loss and alienation. We held court, sometimes for hours, at a gay bar in The Castro called Uncle Bert's, where I learned more of the truth about the gay life from those who lived it than I could ever have gleaned from the pages of any of the books I had been reading on the subject.

Often, during those eight days, while Eddie was eagerly showing me the many wonderful aspects of his life in San Francisco he would say: "Please tell them back home what a good life I've had here. Please tell them what it's *really* like. Make them understand it's not like what they see on television. Tell them how really normal our lives are, that we work hard, play, have pets, plant gardens, are sometimes happy, sometimes sad — just the same as everybody else."

Eddie was right. As I looked around me at San Francisco, and especially at the gay enclave of The Castro, I was struck with the utter normality of the place (not to be confused with "banality," as there is certainly nothing commonplace or mundane about this rarest of jewels among American cities). There was not a thing here to even vaguely suggest a day-to-day way of life similar to the totally depraved existence depicted so graphically in carefully edited videos produced by religious extremist organizations and foisted onto the public as absolute truth. Everyday life in The Castro no more resembles a Gay Pride Parade than daily life in the New Orleans French Quarter corresponds to the revelry of Mardi Gras. All representations to the contrary are simply not true reflections of any kind of meaningful reality.

One evening, late in my stay, a glance at his reflection in a bedroom mirror caused Eddie to collapse suddenly into a flood of anguished tears. He said for a moment he didn't even recognize his own reflection. *Who is that?* was the thought that had first leapt to his mind. The ninety-pound body in the mirror was simply not his any more. "I feel as though I'm just vanishing before my very eyes," he sobbed. "I've watched too many friends waste away like this. I don't think I can bear it. I've seen too much of death for a person my age." I held him until the crying subsided.

Only a year earlier Eddie and nine other friends living with AIDS had formed a breakfast club that met almost every morning for conversation, support and fellowship. Now, death had whittled the breakfast club down to only two members. Before I left for Indiana, Eddie made me promise that after he died I would scatter his ashes at the base of a huge willow tree on his family's farm, where he had spent many happy hours as a youngster.

I bore witness to the terrible suffering, emotional as well as physical, that had been needlessly and cruelly inflicted upon these warm, loving, kind and decent people, and for many weeks after my return to Sunnyside that witness haunted me without ceasing. I could feel the tense uneasiness growing inside me like a malignancy. At night, my dreams were often troubled by the faces of people in pain. Their stories would run over and over in my mind. During the day, I tried hard not to think about it, and concentrated on keeping myself busy. But the things I had seen, the things I had heard, the many bitter realities I had come to know and understand would give me no lasting peace. I was running away, but there was no place to hide.

The birth of my first grandchild intervened and, because of my daughter's extremely difficult delivery, all other considerations were immediately set aside, at least for the time being. I was at Tanya's bedside continuously throughout the excruciating thirteen hours of her labor. Bruce was beside himself with anxiety, being forced to remain in the waiting room because he was considered too young to be with his sister during her delivery. He could only watch fearfully as she was hurriedly taken, screaming in pain, from the maternity ward into surgery for an emergency cesarean procedure.

The next day, however, Bruce was permitted to go to the nursery to have a first look at his tiny niece. The streets of downtown Sunnyside were bustling with activity, the annual German community "Octoberfest" being in full swing. As we made our way through the crowds, I could sense Bruce's excitement and anticipation at getting to see the new baby for the first time. I was in a very agreeable mood myself, having just learned that my granddaughter and I would share the same middle name, "Dawn." The throngs of people and festive atmosphere added to our feelings of good humor and excitement. As we approached the entrance to the hospital, however, a pick-up truck, filled with young men and boys, passed by us on the street. "Faggot!" they all yelled in roaring unison, causing everyone on the sidewalk to turn and stare at us. Like a stone through a stained glass window, our beautiful, joyous day was suddenly shattered by that single word hurled at Bruce in hateful malice.

Rage struck me in the gut like a baseball, momentarily taking my breath. My son couldn't even walk down a public street in his own hometown without being harassed. Now, this wonderful occasion would be tarnished forever by a single act of concerted ugliness.

Bruce stopped dead in his tracks. "Can I respond to that, mom?" he pleaded.

"No, son," I replied, trying desperately to throttle my seething anger. "You know that stooping to their level is not the right way to handle things like this."

I am really not altogether sure exactly what happened after that, but the next thing I knew I was running right down the middle of the street after that truck giving them every obscene gesture I knew (and even a few I didn't know I knew). "Come back here you. . . . you chicken livers," I screamed, "and say that to my face!" (Apparently my vocabulary was not as up to the moment as my body language).

"Look at that crazy bitch!" I heard someone yell, I think from the truck.

Suddenly I just froze. There I was, standing in the middle of the street, horrified and humiliated. All around me people were staring at the public spectacle I had created. Taking a deep breath, and mustering what dignity I had left, I turned and walked stiffly back to where my bewildered son stood on the curb.

"So, I couldn't say anything, huh, mom?" he said, looking a little embarrassed, but mostly amused at his mother's very uncharacteristic display. All I could do was shrug and smile sheepishly.

"But, mom," he queried, returning my shrug, " 'chicken livers'!?"

"It was all I could think of," I said, meekly.

When we returned home, I immediately called my friend Dixie's husband, who is a counselor. "Art," I said, when he picked up the phone, "I'm losing it." And I proceeded to explain what I had done that afternoon.

"Well," Art replied, trying rather unsuccessfully to suppress a chuckle, "you've been under a lot of stress lately. It probably did you good to release a little tension. I wouldn't worry about it if I were you." Then, his sense of humor getting the better of him, he added: "Unless, of course, you get the impulse to run down the middle of the street making obscene gestures every time you see a truck pass by!" With that, we both dissolved into uncontrollable laughter.

For months after that it was a running family joke, whenever we were out together and a truck would pass, that Bruce and Butch would pretend to restrain me. "Oh, no!" Bruce would cry. "It's a truck!" "Hold her back! Hold her back!" Butch would exclaim. My truck-chasing incident has become a piece of Murray family lore, and has been recounted far and wide.

Despite all the excitement and diversion that surrounded the birth of my granddaughter, the new consciousness that had been growing within me since my return from San Francisco did not abate. In every quiet moment it was there waiting to recapture my attention. The small voice that had begun as a persistent whisper in the back of my brain now grew louder, more and more impossible to ignore. I knew that I was rapidly approaching another revelatory turning point. But, whereas the first had brought me peace, the emergence of this new destiny filled me only with apprehension. I did not want to hear what that voice in the back of my head was saying. I did not want my life turned inside out and upside down. I wanted to stay as comfortable as I could with things remaining just the way they were, thank you very much. In reality, however, just how comfortable was I if my own son did not have the freedom to walk down the street without fear of verbal or even physical harassment? That thought, in and of itself, was most discomforting.

I don't know why, exactly, these moments of truth always seem to come upon me in the bathroom. Perhaps it's because it has no windows and is totally pitch dark when the light is turned out, giving a sense of complete isolation. Also, let's face it, it is just about the most private room in the house and the place where one is most likely to find one's self alone. In any case, be all that as it may, my second great struggle with God took place once again in my tiny bathroom. I turned out the light and waited.

What ensued was more like an argument, than anything else. I knew in my soul what was expected of me, all I wanted was to be let off the hook. But God's gay and lesbian children were no longer invisible to me, the way they once had been. I had seen their plight, witnessed their painful struggles with alienation and injustice. I could not turn away from them now. God himself was demanding that I do no less than tell the world.

"You must use your voice, as a Christian, as a mother and as a straight person, to speak their truth," commanded the spirit inside my head, as I sat curled up in a little ball on the floor of my pitch-black bathroom.

"Oh, no, no, not me! Not that!" I protested. "The world will despise me for that. The world will paint me with the same dehumanizing brush as it does the gay people! I'm not ready for that, Lord! I don't want to be a pariah. I haven't the strength for it. — Listen, God," I bargained, "How about if I just feed the hungry and clothe the naked? The world loves people who do those kinds of good deeds. — Or, how about all the orphans and unwed mothers? I could take care of them! Right?! — Oh, please! Oh, please! Give me some other mission, any mission but this one! There must be lots of others who'd be better at this than I would."

I was almost in tears, but it was no use. I knew my own heart would convict me if I continued to turn a deaf ear to the voice of God and conscience. It was clearly a matter of choosing between being hated by the world, or hating myself. My life had become so intertwined with the gay community that their pain had actually become my own, their truth my truth, their struggle my struggle. I simply could not continue to stand silently on the sidelines, a passive observer to their suffering. I must instead bear witness to it. I knew I was being called to share their lot, to step out of the mainstream forever and take my place among society's marginalized. My heart whispered: "You must because you love these people so." Of course I had to surrender. In the end, my love was greater than my fear.

I chose to be hated, marginalized, stigmatized and persecuted because gay people *did not* choose to be those things. I know it is what Christ would do. I made a promise to God that from that moment on I would speak out for his gay and lesbian children whenever and wherever the opportunity presented itself. "Dear Lord," I prayed. "Give me not only the words, but the courage."

CHAPTER XII

      Despite my firm resolve, at first I was a rather reluctant activist. Still, I felt almost as if I were being propelled by some unseen force. Within a matter of weeks my family was presented with the opportunity to take our first wobbly steps as gay activists and educators. We were asked to speak before a teachers' seminar, part of a workshop being held at Indiana University, dealing with the need for sensitivity to the issues and problems facing gay, lesbian and bisexual youth. We were told we did not have to use our real names, which, at the time, Butch, Bruce and I agreed was probably a good idea. I swallowed hard, and told the contact person we'd be there.

      No sooner had I agreed to appear at the seminar than it hit me: What was I going to say? I was not, and am not, a public speaker. In fact, public speaking is my number one phobia. Memories of all those horrible experiences, giving oral presentations in school, flooded my head. I could still hear the snickers and see the mocking faces of my fellow students as I nervously and self-consciously fumbled and stumbled my way through some recitation or book report. Sometimes I would get to trembling so badly that the teacher would stop me for fear I was about to go into convulsions.

      I sat staring at the blank page, trying to put my thoughts together for my presentation, when suddenly a strange thing began to happen; the words just started to flow out of me almost effortlessly. When I had finished, and read over what I had written, I amazed myself. There it was, the story of how my son had struggled throughout his days at school and how I did not want to see other gay and lesbian children suffer as he had done. To me it seemed clear that God had had a hand in writing my first activist talk.

Our car was like a tomb, on the hour's drive from Sunnyside to Bloomington. The stony silence betrayed my family's tension and misgivings about the rapidly approaching turning point in our lives. Today, I sometimes wonder if we would have had the courage to make that first trek into the uncharted territory of social activism had we known where the journey would eventually take us.

Upon our arrival we were greeted quite graciously by the workshop's sponsors. Their obvious gratitude gave me the immediate impression that, even with our phony names, as parents who would stand up for their gay child we were a rare and valuable commodity. I sat at a table before the audience, sandwiched between my husband and son, feeling simultaneously both ashamed and relieved by the alias printed on the name tag affixed to my jacket.

My anxiety mounted as the time approached for me to speak. When I stood up, I felt my knees were insufficient to support me. My hands trembled so that I found it nearly impossible to read from the notes I was holding. When I reached the part of my talk where I narrated the abominable treatment Bruce had been forced to endure at school and in our community, emotion nearly overwhelmed me, and I had to take a moment to compose myself.

I finished my comments by reminding this audience of educators that one of the challenges faced by all parents and teachers is answering the myriad questions children continually pose. "My son raised one that maybe you can help me with," I said. "He knows his very existence is upsetting to many people and that it makes them feel uncomfortable. But he wonders why our society is not at least as troubled and made equally uncomfortable by the hatemongers among us and the countless acts of violence and cruelty they engender against gays and lesbians every day in every city and town across our country. Why is our tolerance for the gay or lesbian in our midst so low while we seemingly possess a limitless capacity to tolerate, or at least ignore, the senseless, unprovoked words and deeds of savage hatred directed toward them? — How would you answer my son?" I inquired.

The room was dead silent. I scanned the audience. Some were wiping tears from their eyes, others avoided my gaze. I glanced over at the young, gay man who had helped to organize the seminar. It was easy to read the gratitude and admiration on his face. His was a look I would see time and again, on the faces of gays and lesbians, as I hesitantly began taking my family's story on the road.

After our presentation there was a question-and-answer period. I surprised myself by my ability to field questions with considerable ease and a sense of quiet confidence. A kind of tranquility appeared to have over-taken me of a sudden, and the answers to questions seemed to come to me effortlessly. What a curious situa-tion, I considered: Here I was, a person who had not even finished high school, educating educators. From the kinds of questions they were asking, it was clear to me that we had given some, in that roomful of teachers, a whole new perspective on the plight of gay and lesbian Americans. Largely because of the example of my family, I'm certain, many in the audience that day were seeing gay people as genuine human beings for the very first time. Presenting gays and lesbians as the real people they truly are is the key to dispelling stereotype-based images of lewd, immoral, subhuman sexual predators so important to the success of the antigay propaganda being churned out by religious and political extremists. For the vision of our shared humanity throws open the door to true empathy, thus inhibiting the capacity for ruthless prejudice to do its dirty work. At the real heart of most objections to the "Love Makes a Family" photo exhibit, for example, is the fact that it presents gays and lesbians as altogether average, almost boring, human beings. It's really very hard to find anything in those pictures of ordinary gay people to be afraid of.

After the seminar we stood at the door as most of the teachers came up to thank us and to share their feelings about the presentation. By and large, their impressions were very favorable. Many hugged us, saying how much they appreciated our courage and how it had given them the long-wished-for opportunity to have a meaningful dialogue about this issue. Some few, however, refused even to look at us, and brushed hurriedly past without even shaking our hands. One woman, I recall, pushed quickly through the door as she mumbled, "Good luck, lady. You're going to need it."

From that day on, an endless stream of opportunities to speak out, educate and advocate began presenting themselves. Our foray into activism was much like crossing a creek by jumping from one stepping stone to another. The stones, however, were not equidistant and each one required a slightly greater leap of faith.

We did an interview for a Louisville television station in which we appeared in shadow. It was strange and exciting to find the anchorwoman, from the evening news program that we watched regularly, sitting in our living room interviewing us. But we had many lessons to learn about the media, some of them not altogether pleasant. We were amazed, for example, that an hour's interview would often be edited down to less than a minute by the time it was broadcast. Sometimes the context of what remained became somewhat distorted, giving the content's meaning an entirely different slant than it originally possessed. Television news is a world of sound bytes, voice-overs and talking heads. The art of the sound byte takes much practice to master, as any successful politician can attest.

Soon, we were doing panels all over Indiana and northern Kentucky for school counselors, teacher's associations, law enforcement, PFLAG chapters and organizations for lesbian and gay teens. I continued to battle the stage fright that often kept me awake for nights on end prior to an appearance, and would sometimes even result in my becoming physically ill. At times I would begin to wonder why I put myself through such personal torture. Then some grateful mother would come up to me after a presentation and tell me about her gay child's ordeal and thank me for having the courage to speak up, thereby reminding me *exactly* why I was doing what I was doing. Sometimes, several days after an appearance, I'd get a letter from a lesbian or gay man who told me they had been in complete despair, near the brink of suicide, but my words had given them hope. It was this kind of "shot in the arm" that, more than once, was all that kept me going.

Wishing to acclimate myself to seeing and hearing about gay men openly expressing physical affection for each other, I had ordered a subscription to *Genre* magazine. I wanted to be able to share fully in Bruce's life. I wanted him to feel completely free to express all the joy and excitement that only romantic love can evoke, without witnessing even the slightest trace of discomfort on my part in so doing. When you fall in love it is such pure delight to be able to tell someone just how wonderful your lover is and how gloriously happy you are. I wanted to be that someone for Bruce, should he choose me to be. I studied the advertisements and photos in *Genre,* which often depicted men caressing each other or in warm, loving embraces. But all I could see was human tenderness and sexuality. What was there here to find disgusting or offensive? Must our images of men's behavior toward each other *always* involve some element of unyielding aggressiveness, competitiveness or belligerence in order to be acceptable to our eyes? Do the limits of intimate friendship between males always have to be defined by a kind of jocular camaraderie? Even though, because of my love for my son, I had some predilection to do so, I was still rather surprised at how easy it was for me to accept seeing such contact between males, despite an upbringing which dictated that nearly all physical acts of affection between men must be considered taboo, or, at the very least, suspect.

One night I got a sudden, pressing urge to share my insights concerning intermale affection with the readers of *Genre*. I sat down and wrote a letter to the editors.

My letter was published the following month under the slightly perplexing title of "Mommy Dearest," along with my name and where I was from. In the weeks that followed I began receiving letters from all across the country from gay men who were touched by my accepting, unconditional commitment to my son. One letter in particular stood apart from the rest. It described a tortured life lived through years of denial, a failed marriage and a nearly successful suicide attempt. That letter was from a former member of my church, and it gave me a distinct feeling of spiritual connectedness and the sense that my urgent need to communicate with other readers of *Genre* magazine was somehow divinely inspired.

Two years after my letter was published, I was still witnessing its impact. While reading over the obituaries, in the local newspaper, I noticed that the son of my doctor's former nurse had died of AIDS. The young man had long ago moved to New York City. I felt I must contact his mother and offer whatever words of comfort I could, but I didn't know how to approach her. Such an obituary in the Sunnyside paper could represent either a mother's very courageous statement or the act of some malicious local scandalmonger. There was no way of knowing, from the article on the obituary page, how this woman might feel concerning her new visibility in the community. I bought a bouquet of flowers and, as I drove to the woman's house through a pouring rain, prayed for the right words to say to her.

When she opened the front door, I must have been a sight to behold standing there soaking wet on her front porch clutching a bunch of flowers. I said: "Mrs. Anderson, I don't know if you remember me, but . . ."

"Yes, yes, of course, my dear," she interrupted, with a bright smile. "Mrs. Murray, do come in here out of the rain."

She ushered me into her tidy living room and accepted the dripping flowers. Mrs. Anderson took my cold, wet hand warmly in hers for a moment. "I hear we have something in common," she said. "My Bob was one of God's precious gay children like your son, Bruce. Two years ago, my son sent me a copy of the letter you had written to *Genre* magazine. Last Sunday I stood up in church and announced to them all that it was true my Bob had died of AIDS. I declared he was a good person, a child of God and worthy of love. — Now, I want to meet your son and tell him the same."

I was dumbfounded. Here I had come with a troubled heart, not having the vaguest notion of how to initiate a conversation with this wonderful, kind and loving woman, when in fact the conversation had already been initiated two years earlier. It was clear to me then and there that I had received divine guidance when I wrote that letter.

Mrs. Anderson did come to our home. She read scripture for Bruce, kissed him and told him to always remember that he was precious to God. She reminded my son that he could do anything he chose to in his life because he was truly blessed.

Bruce was overwhelmed. After she left, I told him to balance the picture of hatred that he had received from his church with the wonderful love of this woman. For she was indeed a representative of the true Christ.

I had been corresponding with the minister who had been our interim pastor between the departure of Rev. Smith and the arrival of Mark Roberts. He was a kind and gracious man, who always found time to listen and comfort. In my 1994 Christmas card, I told him where I now stood in my journey. To my surprise, I received a copy of the sermon he had preached to his large Austin, Texas congregation the previous Sunday. I was quite astonished to read my own words mirrored back at me. The sermon began:

"Recently, I received a letter from a dear friend who has been struggling over the fact that her teenage son is gay. In her letter she wrote: 'For over a year, Paul, I hadn't felt God's presence. I would pray and there was this silence. I would sit in the pew every Sunday and worship and be involved in church projects of every kind, but still this dreaded silence. I begged, I pleaded and bargained with God . . . only crushing silence. Now I know God was speaking to me through his silence. He wanted me to let go of my old ways so I would be ready to encounter Him in the strangest places. God has used my experience with my son. Paul, I have a lot of beautiful, wonderful gay children now who like to call me "mom." They flock around me just to spend a few moments with me because they are thirsting for acceptance without judgement and love without condition. I know I represent what they wish from their own families. But I don't believe they know how they are healing me. For the more I empty myself of my fear and prejudice, the more I am filled with peace and happiness. When I reach out and touch the untouchable, I find Christ. I never knew what a hug could mean until I received one from a person dying with AIDS. When I found myself loving those I had always been taught were unlovable, I discovered love for the one whom I really *believed* to be unlovable, me. In my blindness, I thought I was losing a son, but now I know I am encountering God's son! I am overwhelmed with God's presence. In the midst of suffering, violence, and hatred I have found such joy and love. Much to my surprise, I have found myself dancing in society's margins, dancing with the "Lord of the Dance." I must seem pretty strange to onlookers, who can't hear the music, but, Paul, don't you just love that beat?! Doesn't it make you want to dance wherever you may be?' "

Attached to the sermon was a note from a mother who had been sitting in the congregation that Sunday morning. She had only recently learned that her teenage son was gay. My letter had deeply moved a person, over a thousand miles away, who was a complete stranger to me. I was beginning to believe in the power of the word and its ability to subdue the troubled heart and conquer the deadly sword.

Bruce and I were becoming quite an activist team. Some affectionately referred to us as "the Judds of the gay community" (for those unfamiliar with country music, The Judds are a mother-daughter singing team). We were kept very busy lecturing and participating in panel discussions at Indiana University and The University of Louisville.

Graduate students from I.U. approached us to be part of a video presentation scheduled to air on WTIU, the local PBS affiliate. This time we did not appear in shadow and our real names were used. Such high-profile visibility represented one of our bigger leaps toward activism. After the piece was broadcast we held our breath, waiting for community reaction. We received a few vulgar phone calls, mostly from what sounded like teenage boys. For the most part we got dirty looks from people on the street, whispers behind our backs and general shunning. But the thrust of courage that it had taken to do the broadcast made us stronger as a family. We no longer looked above people's heads, or over their shoulders when we met them. We made eye contact, smiled and said "hello."

As a parent, I was constantly struggling with becoming too conspicuous as a gay activist and thereby putting my family at risk. Bruce and I had long conversations about the dangers of our growing visibility. "Mom, I refuse to live my life in fear any longer," he said. "That is what your example has taught me, and that is what I believe."

One night, shortly after the public TV appearance, Bruce was driving home alone through the country when suddenly he saw the flashing red and blue lights of a police car appear in his rear-view mirror. He hadn't been speeding and couldn't think of any reason why a policeman should be stopping him. Apprehensively, Bruce guided the car to a stop on the shoulder and waited for the Indiana State Trooper to approach.

"What seems to be the problem, officer?" Bruce asked, rolling down the window.

"License and registration," the trooper sternly replied. He studied the picture on the driver's license, then shone his flashlight directly on Bruce's face. "Say, you look familiar. Don't I know you from somewhere? — Yeah, I know where I've seen you. It was on television the other night. You're the kid from that show about gays, aren't you?"

Bruce looked up and nodded self-consciously. Here he was on a dark country road in the middle of the night, stopped by a burly state policeman who had just realized Bruce was gay. All the stereotypes pointed to the conclusion that nothing good could possibly come from this situation.

"Well," said the officer, smiling broadly as he handed Bruce's documents back to him. "Good job, son. You just keep movin' along now, but be careful. There's a lot of animals sometimes run out in your road. Don't put yourself in the ditch tryin' to avoid one. — Oh, and by the way. You've got a tail light out back there on the right side. Better get it fixed 'fore you get a ticket."

At a shopping mall, a few days later, however, Bruce had an encounter with a perfect stranger that proved to be not quite so fortunate. Out of the blue, a large man strode directly up to him, screamed the words, "Goddamn faggot," and slapped Bruce directly across the face. He then turned and quickly vanished.

Another disturbing, though not directly violent, incident occurred in the clothing store where Bruce worked. He had noticed a woman customer who seemed to linger about, watching him anxiously. After the store had cleared of other customers, she hesitantly approached Bruce. She said she had seen him on television, and told him his courage was very admirable. "But you must be very careful," the woman whispered, nervously. "You see, my son was gay too. — A beautiful young man, he was, like you.

— He's dead now." She hesitated a moment, struggling, with obvious anguish, to stifle her raging emotions. "A gang of boys beat him to death with baseball bats," she finally blurted, and with that, burst into tears. Before Bruce could do anything to comfort her, the woman ran hysterically from the store. He's never seen her again.

One day I received a call from Zoe Hudson, Assistant Director of Communications for the national PFLAG office in Washington, DC. She wanted to know if Bruce and I would be willing to participate in a press conference PFLAG was organizing prior to the so-called Hoekstra Congressional Hearings. These "hearings," held before Rep. Hoekstra's Congressional Committee, purported to deal with education, parents' rights, and family values. In reality, however, they were little more than a high-profile forum for airing the bigoted views of Mr. Hoekstra's friend, the Rev. Lou Sheldon. A cornerstone of Rev. Sheldon's agenda is the total elimination of any and all support for gay and lesbian students from the public schools. I told Zoe I would have to talk it over with Bruce before I could give her an answer.

That evening Bruce gaped at me in disbelief, as I explained Zoe's proposal to him. "Well, I say we go for it!" he declared, after the initial shock had worn off.

"I was hoping you'd say that," I replied, with a grin.

A few short days later, we found ourselves aboard an airliner headed for Washington, guests of the Human Rights Campaign. It was our first visit to the nation's capital, and we were both too excited for words. Zoe met our flight and delivered us to our downtown hotel, telling us to be at PFLAG's offices at 9:00 sharp the following morning.

Bruce and I stared at each other across the space separating the two double beds in the hotel room. We still found it hard to believe we were actually in Washington, DC, and were going to be doing a press conference in the morning! It felt like a dream. We tried rehearsing our statements, but nervous excitement wouldn't let us. All of a sudden I jumped in the middle of my bed and started bouncing, back and forth, from one bed to the other like some six-year-old. Laughing, Bruce followed suit. We bounced and teased and chased each other about the room until we collapsed, exhausted and laughing crazily, on the floor. After recovering from our horseplay, we found it was now possible for us to practice our statements.

It was altogether impossible for me to sleep that night. I lay awake staring at the ceiling, contemplating how much my life had changed in just a few short months, and how unreal it all seemed now. One thing was certain, there would be no turning back after tomorrow. The course would be clearly set after that.

Eating breakfast was unthinkable for both of us. Food just didn't seem the least bit interesting. When we arrived at PFLAG headquarters we were met at the door by Zoe, and Communications Director Rob Banaszak. To laid-back heartlanders like us, Rob and Zoe were real human dynamos, juggling hundreds of ideas, people, commitments and responsibilities all at once, their bustling feet seemingly always three inches above the floor. The intense energy and enthusiasm they exhibited truly astounded us small-town yokels, who were more accustomed to life in the slow lane. Still, no matter how hectic things became, either Rob or Zoe or both of them would always be near our sides to tend to Bruce's or my smallest concern or question. They gave us reams of briefing materials and fact sheets, asking us to review them. Then we were whisked off to their public relations firm, where we were warned about how people from the press might try to sidetrack us, and that we must control the interviews by sticking to the issues at hand. They also encouraged us to organize our thoughts in terms of sound bytes. To calm our jangled nerves a bit, after leaving the agency, Rob took us to a nearby Au Bon Pain Restaurant to relax for a few minutes over tea and coffee.

Then we were off again. Next stop was the headquarters of The Human Rights Campaign. Again, walking in off the street, we were immediately transported into a place where the very atmosphere seemed electrically charged by the intense passion and zeal of those who worked there. Zoe sensed that Bruce and I were beginning to feel a little overwhelmed. At that point, I think Zoe and Rob were becoming apprehensive that we might bolt.

"Bruce, you were so talkative on the phone," Zoe said. "Now you're so quiet. What's the matter?"

"Oh, I get a little quiet when I'm nervous, " he replied.

I think she was afraid Bruce would freeze up during the press conference, and frankly, at that particular juncture, I wasn't at all sure he wouldn't. I wasn't at all sure that *I* wouldn't, as a matter of fact.

Next, we had a meeting with representatives from the National Gay and Lesbian Task Force, People for the American Way, the National Organization for Women, The Triangle, and several others. We were seated at the head of a long table. Basically, what these gay and gay-friendly organizations wanted to know was what we were going to say to the media. They subjected Bruce and me to a series of rapid-fire questions, and I remember thinking at the time that the press conference itself could not possibly be any worse than this. I got up to go to the restroom when Zoe said: "Rhea, you can leave your coat here." By the look on her face, I could tell she was afraid I would flee the building, head straight for the airport and take the very next plane bound for Indianapolis. She may well have been right, the tension was mounting so by that point. In any case, just to be on the safe side, she followed me to the restroom door.

From HRC headquarters we were taken to the Rayburn House Office Building. As the press conference got under way, Bruce and I exchanged brief glances of desperation. When I got up to speak, he squeezed my hand for comfort. With my son at my side, I made my statement deploring the use of a congressional committee for the purpose of furthering the political and social agenda of extremists and bigots, whose only purpose in life was to spread lies and half-truths about gay people. I did my best to explain the dreadful realities of raising an openly gay child in a country so overwhelmingly dominated by mindless hostility, prejudice and unfettered hatred toward lesbian, gay and bisexual people. Amazingly, during the entire meeting, all I could think about was my love for my son. That was what sustained me and kept me going. I forgot about my fear and nervousness by concentrating on the love I felt for Bruce. When I finished my statement, I looked out over the audience. I could read concern and sorrow on many of the faces before me. That entire room bore witness to the love and dedication that my child and I have for each other, and the courage it has engendered in both of us.

Then it was Bruce's turn to speak. Unbeknownst to Zoe, I had told him to pause for a few seconds before starting in order to compose himself. He did just that, scanning the audience silently before he spoke. A look of sheer terror crossed Zoe's face. I learned from her later that in those few seconds, she had been certain Bruce had frozen. Then he began to speak in a clear, calm, forthright manner. Tears flooded my eyes, rolled down my cheeks and dropped onto my folded hands, as I watched my brave son address the media. I was filled with pride for him because in spite of all the terrible things that had happened to Bruce, his courage had carried him through, and now here he was fearlessly telling his story for all to hear. In truth this is the real meaning of "gay pride." It is the strength of character and the self-esteem that come from surviving, enduring and succeeding despite the intense efforts of a veritable army of those who would demean, and indeed destroy, gay people.

Immediately following our initial statements to the press we were pulled aside to be interviewed by various representatives of radio and television networks. Rob Banaszak stayed protectively close by us. He was not about to let the press eat us alive. Rob and Zoe were our guardian angels during the entire Washington experience. We have remained close friends. I still often hear from Rob, either by e-mail or telephone, several times per week.

After the radio and TV interviews, Bruce and I were hurried off, by Mike Roybal of the Human Rights Campaign, to do a drop-by lobbying visit to Representative Tim Roemer's office. As the mother of a gay child, I pleaded with one of Roemer's assistants for the congress of my country to be more aware of the needless suffering that their ugly, divisive, and usually politically motivated debates over gay issues can cause families like mine. The aid told me that it was most unfortunate, but in the vicious environment in which public discourse is conducted today, questions of gay civil rights were simply the manna upon which the political beast must feed. I said to him: "No, sir, you are wrong there. It is my child that the politicians are feeding on. My child is their manna. There are human beings involved here, not just faceless issues." By the end of the day I had acquired the nickname, Mrs. Soundbyte. After our work was finished, Mike Roybal took us on a tour of the Capitol building. He said he also wanted to show us The Mall. "Oh, goody!" we squealed. "Now we can get down to some serious shopping!"

When Rob saw us off at the airport, he hugged me and said, "I love you, my Indiana mom." That is how closely we had bonded in the short time we spent together. Our three-day stay in Washington was at once the most terrifying, fascinating and magical time of my life. Both Bruce and I fell in love with our nation's beautiful capital city and all the many wonderful people we met while we were there. It was an experience we shall never forget.

CHAPTER XIII

We were so involved in our various support groups and educational programs that sometimes our home seemed only to be a place where we occasionally dropped by for meals, to change clothes and to sleep. One afternoon, over coffee and cookies, I complained to my good friend, Dixie, about the long hours we were spending on the road. She asked me if I had ever considered the idea of starting a PFLAG chapter in Sunnyside.

"Oh, yeah, right!" I laughed. "Get real, Dixie. A PFLAG chapter in Sunnyside, Indiana!?"

But my friend persisted, and I soon realized she was not pulling my leg. Dixie was dead serious! "Rhea, you know there have to be other families around here that have gone through, or are going through, the same thing your family has. Think of what it would have meant to you and your family, in your darkest moments, if you had had someplace to turn right here in your own home town, instead of having to search for weeks for support groups. Then, even after you found them, you had to drive over an hour each way to get to the meetings."

"But, Dixie," I protested. "Where in the wide world would I ever even begin? We have no gay network of any kind in this area. In fact, the gays and lesbians who live around here are even isolated from each other. There's no gay-friendly church, not even a viable, welcoming counseling service. There's no human rights council. I would have absolutely zero community support. I'd be lucky not to be given a ride out of this town on that well-known rail!"

Dixie continued gently to coax and cajole me. She said that in larger communities PFLAG was only one link in a broader support network for gays and lesbians and their families. In Sunnyside, however, it would be the *only* support. I soon came to realize that all the reasons why it would be difficult to establish a chapter in our town were the exact reasons why we needed one. I decided to go for it.

One of the first obstacles I faced was how to get the word out without exposing my family to any increased danger from the numerous hostile elements in the community. Using a post-office box for an address, I had some calling cards printed up. I didn't have the money to have a separate PFLAG phone line connected, so I had to take the risk of having my own number printed on the cards. Boldly demonstrating the courage of her own convictions, Dixie agreed to be a contact person as well, and her number was placed on the cards below mine. Next, I distributed a letter introducing myself and PFLAG to all professional counselors, psychologists and psychiatrists in the counties surrounding Sunnyside.

When I went to a local printer, to have my cards printed and the letter duplicated, I could sense the great discomfort of the people who worked there. I tried to act casual and relaxed in order to put them at their ease, but I could tell it wasn't working. I learned, through the beauty-parlor grapevine, a few days later, that a rumor was circulating around town to the effect that I was a lesbian who was starting a gay dance club called P-FAG! This preposterous blab only made me laugh, but my mother, for one, was not quite so amused. In fact, she was deeply upset and anxious for my safety.

I knew the origin of the rumors had to be in the print shop, so I decided to deal with the problem at its source. When I went in to pick up my finished calling cards, I engaged the clerk in casual, friendly conversation. "You know," I said, looking at her and smiling, "I'd like to explain what my organization is all about." I proceeded to briefly narrate the story of my family's long, arduous struggle, and told her we wanted to help others who found themselves on a similar journey to avoid some of the pitfalls we had encountered along the way "So," I sighed at last, "if you hear anyone inquiring after my organization, please let them know what we're all about. — You know, it's funny, I've even heard rumors that I'm a lesbian who is starting some sort of gay dance club, or something like that," I laughed.

The woman flushed immediately, and actually admitted that she was the one who had started the gossip about me. "I'm sorry," she said. "I didn't have any idea."

"It's all right, honey," I replied, gently patting her arm. "Our fears can very often make us jump to the wrong conclusions." I figured it made more sense to try to build some bridges, than to go in there busting down doors.

Since the most common meeting place for PFLAG chapters is in gay-friendly churches, I was at a loss as to where to hold our meetings. Initially, it would have to be our home that served as the gathering place. That would mean, of course, placing my family at greater risk, but for the time being that simply couldn't be helped. It would be necessary to carefully screen all the telephone calls before revealing the location of the meetings. I announced the date for the first get-together, and held my breath.

I told myself not to expect too much of the opening meeting. After all, there had only been five present at the first PFLAG gathering in Louisville, Kentucky, a metropolitan area a hundred times the size of Sunnyside. I must admit, as the inaugural date approached, I was preparing myself for a disastrous failure. Imagine my delighted surprise, then, when ten brave souls showed up at my door on that first day! Within a year our monthly attendance had increased to thirty regular participants, with a mailing list that includes fifty families.

Our meetings rapidly grew too large for our small home, but I soon discovered that the local public library was willing to allow us the use of their spacious conference room on Sunday afternoons. The chapter's membership consists half of gays and lesbians, with the other half being made up of straight supporters. Unfortunately, as of this writing, Butch and I are still the only parents of a gay child in attendance. Though we have been secretly approached by several parents from the Sunnyside area, who have told us that they appreciate our work on behalf of their gay children and how much they admire us for our courage, none of these dads and moms have been willing to join directly in the activities of the group. Sadly, their fear keeps them on the sidelines and restrains them from greater understanding, not only of their gay and lesbian offspring, but of their own feelings and misconceptions about homosexuality as well. I must admit that this situation has been for me, at times, something of a bitter pill to swallow. Here my husband and I are, willing to take it on the chin from the homophobic bigots that surround us on every side, while these parents of gay and lesbian kids doggedly insist on remaining in the shadows, frozen in their silent fear.

The love and gratitude I have received from gay men and lesbians who live in and around Sunnyside has more than made up for the verbal buffeting I sometimes get from reactionary extremists in the community as well as the general lack of visible support from parents. These gay folks have been so thrilled to find that a place for them to turn is actually emerging in their small-town, rural community that something approaching an awakening has begun to take place. It is so heart-warming to see them (if a little tentatively at first) making new friends among themselves and beginning to socialize with each other outside of the PFLAG meetings. Many have gained a new sense of self-worth and pride in who they are, and have actually gathered the courage to come out to straight friends and family. For the first time ever, people in Sunnyside, Indiana are beginning to find themselves faced with having to deal, in meaningful ways, with gay people. Gradually, ever so gradually, things are starting to change.

Often, Bruce's former classmates visit the clothing store where he works and are usually friendly with him. Recently, on a few occasions some of his former tormentors have also come round to apologize to him for their past behavior. There are those who have said they were genuinely ashamed for the way they had acted toward him in the past. They knew it was wrong, even at the time it was happening, but just didn't have the guts to go against the flow, when several in their peer group had decided to make a "queer" the target of their scornful contempt. My son's infinite capacity for compassion makes me feel like I want to be just like him when, and if, I ever grow up. He has forgiven them all.

Bruce has actually started to build friendships once again right here in his hometown. That lonely boy who used to spend hours by himself in his room, seemingly totally isolated from the world and in utter despair, has vanished without a trace. The new Bruce is a self-assured young man with friends who seek out his company, dropping by the house at all hours. How dramatically his life has changed! Bruce's new-found sense of pride and self-confidence has transformed him. No longer the victim, he has become the victor in his friends' eyes as well as his own.

In the summer of 1995, Bruce was selected to attend the National Gay and Lesbian Task Force's Youth Institute in San Francisco. There he spent a week with other young gay people, receiving training on how to be more effective as an organizer and activist. He met people who taught him things that had a profound influence on him. The entire experience was very empowering. He left home still a boy, but returned to us as a man with a solid sense of his own self-worth, power, and ability to lead and influence. You could hear it in his voice and see it in his step and the way he carried himself when he walked. I think, perhaps for the first time, he had come to truly like himself.

All of this, of course, is not to say that we don't still have those moments that remind us we are surrounded by homophobes, bigots and the arrogant practitioners of raw, senseless hatred. Things are changing, but that change seems sometimes to be traveling at a snail's pace. I remember seeing a pick-up truck a while back, for example, with a sticker in the rear window that read, "If you are not like me, then I hate you." What struck me about this was not the sentiment itself (if that is indeed what one would call it), but rather the fact that the driver was obviously so proud of his rabid persuasion he felt called upon to plaster it across the back of his truck for all the world to see. Then there was the night that Bruce, white and breathless with terror, burst into the house. He had been driving home after working late, when suddenly a vehicle came rushing up behind him. Bruce could see the headlights glaring in his rear-view mirror as the truck bore down on him. Suddenly he felt a thud as his car was struck from behind by the other vehicle, then another, harder jolt, then another and another. Bruce sped up, but the truck stayed with him. The two vehicles careened perilously down the highway at a high rate of speed. Thinking quickly, Bruce made a sudden left turn onto a side road, nearly landing in the ditch. The turn was too sharp for the truck. It could not follow, but rushed wildly on down the main road, its horn blaring into the night.

One afternoon Bruce came home and sat me down at the dining-room table. "We have to have a serious talk," he said. "Mom, I had lunch today with a girl I used to know back at school. She's the editor of the high-school newspaper. She was browsing the world-wide-web and came across the piece that the Philadelphia Daily News did about us a couple of weeks back, after we were in Washington. — Mom, she wants to interview you and me for an article in the school paper."

A sudden tremor of fear went through me. This was more frightening, and potentially far more dangerous, than even the news conference in Washington, DC. It was anyone's guess how the community might react to reading our story in the high-school newspaper. "What do you want to do about it, son?" I asked, trying not to let my mounting anxiety show too much.

"I'm really torn," he replied. "I am afraid, but I also want them to understand that I'm no longer a victim. — Still, the thought of entering that school again almost makes me physically ill."

Despite all our fears and queasiness, however, the very next day my son and I found ourselves making our way up the walk toward Sunnyside High School. Entering the front door was like revisiting a nightmare. All the bitter pain incurred by the injustices and indignities of two years earlier came rushing back at us. I heard Bruce take a deep breath, and felt the tears welling up in my eyes. But when I looked at him it was clear that this was not the same person who had been so unfairly despised, victimized and humiliated in the presence of these same school-house walls. He stood erect, tall and triumphant, and there was an almost fierce look of intense determination upon his face. I have never been prouder of him.

The interview went smoothly. The student staff of the paper was very polite and cordial to us. Their questions were well balanced, thoughtful and unbiased. There wasn't even a trace of confrontation.

When Friday finally rolled around, and our picture and story appeared on page one with the headline, "Teen Fights For Gay Rights," we waited expectantly for the first obscene phone calls to come in. What ensued, however, was nothing but deafening silence. We were grateful there was no general outcry of protest against the story, but there were no calls of support either. At the school itself, however, things were different. Students tore our picture from the paper and taped it to the walls with little cartoon-strip balloons over our heads indicating our saying such crude and vulgar things as: "I like sucking cock," over Bruce, and "I'm so proud of my faggy son," over me.

The day the story appeared we received a card from the student editor that read:

Dear Rhea and Bruce,
    Thank you so much for taking the time out of your busy day for an interview. I learned so many things by talking to you both. I hope you will be pleased with the final article. I took the position that both of you are working for equal rights for gays and lesbians, and not for "special rights." We plan on doing a follow-up on the harassment issue. I will be contacting you again, if that's O.K. Your story has touched my heart and the hearts of the staff of the paper. You have opened our eyes and our minds. Good luck on your journey.

I deeply admired the courage that I knew it took for these young people to undertake and publish what was quite a sympathetic article about Bruce and me. They took a lot of flack from their peers as well as a few teachers over the piece. But these brave student journalists remembered that if Bruce hadn't been virtually hounded out of the school he would have been graduating with them in just a few short weeks.

The paper's next issue brought a flood of negative letters-to-the-editor from outraged parents and students. One I remember in particular was signed by an entire family, who declared their moral outrage and righteous indignation that such an "obscene" article would ever appear in the student newspaper, especially right on the front page! We took heart, however, from one extremely supportive letter written by a counselor at the high school. For in writing her letter, she was letting every gay and lesbian student know that they had someone they could turn to in the school system for support and guidance. This brave counselor's letter alone balanced out all the many negative ones.

One of Butch's fellow workers had the article duplicated and, in an unmistakable effort to stir up trouble on the job for my husband, distributed the copies to numerous other workers throughout the plant. (There's nothing quite like being outed in a totally blue-collar world. I wouldn't recommend it for the faint of heart.) One of Butch's former bosses was so consumed with irate bigotry over the article that he went straight to the supervisor of the division where my husband now works, insisting that Butch should at least be somehow reprimanded, if not worse. Butch's supervisor, who is from England, glanced at the clipping and shrugged, saying he'd already seen it. When the other man persisted impatiently, the supervisor said: "The man's the boy's father, for heaven's sake. Shouldn't a father be expected to stand behind his own son? I, for one, don't have any problem with that, and I suggest that you shouldn't either."

One of the most personally moving things that happened, following the publication of our interview, came in the form of a letter to Bruce from one of his grade-school teachers:

Dear Bruce,
A teacher friend handed me a recent copy of the high school's paper. She thought I should read the front-page article since you had been in my second grade class years ago (and I still miss you!).
My first reaction was a smile, and then I wished you were there for me to give you a big hug. Bruce, way back when, I can recall being so touched by your sensitivity, your caring nature and your warmth. I worried, even then, thinking that somewhere down the line, people would "mark" you because you were kind, loving and compassionate — very unlike your typical macho, don't-ever-cry kind of guy.
I want you to know that I admire you for speaking out for gay rights. I applaud you for your perseverance. It makes me sad to think that you had to leave the high school because of the discrimination against you. From what I hear,

you could be a gentle voice for gay rights over there right now. Apparently, there have been some rather militant gay gangs, which I think only heightens the discrimination and negative attitudes toward gays. Anger and fights don't gain acceptance.

Bruce, I believe pursuing acceptance for gays is a challenge that you seem ready to face. As your old, graying, second grade teacher, may I add that we, as a people, need to accept boys and men who are kind, sensitive and loving. If a young boy is not a sports freak who eats nails for breakfast, society labels him "different" — even at that early age. My personal feeling is that we need to fight for overall acceptance. Each of us is unique. Each of us is designed by God. You are precious, and don't ever forget that, Bruce.

One of my best friends from high school is a gay man who lives in the Chicago area. My dear uncle, who was gay, died recently from AIDS. I tell you this because I want you to know that I wish you had been around years ago to stand up for these dear men in my life.

I could go on and on. Just know that I am thinking about you and I admire your mother for standing by you. That is what we, as mothers, do. We love our children. As a teacher, I also love my students.

Take good care, Bruce.

With love,
Mrs. Noel

Bruce's 18th birthday arrived in the middle of graduation week, 1996. I knew it was a difficult time for him, not being able to graduate with his class. So, I planned a special evening. I found out that if I signed for Bruce as a sponsor he could go to a huge gay dance club in Louisville called "Connections." So, Butch and I planned a birthday outing with some of Bruce's friends, and a few of ours too.

When he found out that his parents were going to take him to his first gay bar, Bruce was simply flabbergasted. Gloom immediately evaporated from his face like dew off a rose in the bright morning sun. His excitement was infectious, as we walked into the plushly appointed club. I was immediately impressed with the decor and energetic atmosphere. Bruce and I strolled up to the bar, where a handsome young bartender stood waiting to serve us.

"Hello! I'm his mother," I said, indicating Bruce. "We're here celebrating his eighteenth birthday. I've never been here before. — This place is huge! Could you explain the layout, young man?"

I noticed the bartender appeared somewhat nervous. He cleared his throat several times and made a few false starts before he was able to say: "Ma'am, you *do* realize that this *is* a gay bar, don't you?"

"A gay bar! Did you say a gay bar?!!! — Son!" I bellowed, turning dramatically to Bruce. "What on earth are you trying to tell me?!"

The bartender looked as though he'd just seen the ghost of Mae West glide by, his eyes were the size of silver dollars and all the color had drained from his face. Bruce, unable to contain himself any longer, burst into laughter at the young fellow's expression of horrified consternation.

Realizing the joke was on him, the barman's face suddenly broke into a broad, embarrassed grin. "Ah, lady," he said, shyly. "Please don't do that to me. You nearly gave me a heart attack!"

My son and I proceeded from there to take the floor, where we danced the night away. I've rarely felt so completely free, before or since.

CHAPTER XIV

Life for the Murray family seems, in many ways, to have come full circle. The interview published in the high-school paper gave us the opportunity to face many of our past demons head-on. After hearing our story, at one of our classroom presentations, someone complained to the Presbytery about how our family had been treated by our former minister. A response team was organized to check into the situation in hopes of increasing Rev. Roberts' sensitivity to the problems and issues facing gay people and their families. Sadly, the Church's so-called investigation quickly deteriorated into little more than a desperate cover-up, in an attempt to protect a culpable pastor and defend its own callously uncharitable official position regarding the third-class status of gays and lesbians within the Presbyterian community.

Despite Rev. Roberts' grim prediction that no local congregation would ever accept us, we have found a small Episcopal church that has welcomed us with open arms. I had heard a few rumors that this parish might be more accepting. Still, after many months of ostracism, we remained uncertain as to whether we were ready to once again embrace organized religion. We had painful scars, which had only just recently begun to heal. Furthermore, after having come through the most difficult and challenging period of our lives without the love and support of a religious community, it was hard for us to justify any real need for the church. One bright, sunny Sunday morning, however, Butch and I decided to take the chance.

I'm certain the vicar will never forget our first Sunday at his little, rural church. He was receiving members of his congregation near the front door at the conclusion of services. As I approached he gave me a broad, friendly smile.

Grasping Rev. Nigel's out-stretched hand I said: "Hi! We're the Murrays. We have a teenaged gay son whom we love and are very supportive of. Our former pastor told us no church would welcome us. Is that true?"

Much to the good vicar's credit, he was only addled momentarily by my plainspoken candor. Then the smile spread even more broadly across his face. He squeezed my hand tightly and answered: "You and your son are most welcome here any time."

Weeks later we joked about my abrupt introduction. I laughingly, but quite truthfully, told our new pastor that I simply did not want to waste a lot of Sunday mornings trying to find out whether or not there was a place for us in his parish. As it turned out, the vicar's words have been borne out by the warm and welcoming actions of the whole congregation. We have once again found a home in the church.

Often we have encountered people who *say* they are affirming, but their actions, or lack thereof, tell a different story. When you pour your heart out to another person, for example, you expect a bit more than cold, numbing silence in return. This tiny Episcopal congregation has proven their acceptance by actually initiating dialogue with us concerning our lives. Pronouncing the word "gay" itself has not been a problem for them. Some have even brought newspaper and magazine articles concerning gay-rights issues to our attention, with a desire to discuss them with us openly and candidly. Their eagerness to undertake a Sunday-morning forum in which homosexuality was talked about with frankness and compassion completely amazed me. These are people whose hearts have been liberated from the fear of gays and lesbians, and they are therefore prepared to be accepting, understanding and loving. Unfortunately, the pain inflicted upon our son by our former congregation has not healed sufficiently to permit him to attend. Perhaps someday he will be able to look into his heart and find those wounds have vanished, allowing him to come back to the church. Sadly, however, such deep emotional lacerations often leave permanent scars that never disappear completely. I fervently hope and pray this will not be the case for Bruce.

I have had several long, theological discussions with Rev. Nigel in which I've expressed my total unwillingness to return to the blindly accepting religious beliefs of my past. I will always have a questioning faith that leaves room for many voices to speak to me. I will never re-erect those walls of religion that have cut me off from my ability and desire to see myself and others as simply "us," rather than the divisive "us and them." My confirmation as an Episcopalian must be a starting point of faith, not its conclusion. The vicar has assured me that the Episcopal Church allows room for one's faith to grow through personal experience.

Life for me remains a veritable constant flurry of activity. No matter how full my schedule, I do not seem to have it in me to reject an opportunity to bring my family's story to others, so that they will not have to make the same lonely journey we did. My quest of human understanding and acceptance for gays and lesbians has taken me to many diverse cities and towns across our nation. Everywhere I go I encounter throngs of people who want and need to share their painful stories. They open their hearts to me, and I try to support and comfort each one as best I can. I am often overwhelmed by their gratitude, which I find at once touching and quite humbling. Often I am deeply saddened by these encounters as well. The many emotional outpourings I've encountered have nothing to do with me as an individual. Rather, these fine people are so deeply motivated by their need for, and gross lack of, validation and affirmation that they exult in a complete stranger, like me, who is simply willing to say that they are good souls, altogether worthy of love and understanding.

Butch says that I am a lot better at dealing with hostility than I am the tidal waves of love and adoration that often flow my way, and he's right. Once, during Gay Pride Week, I was asked to be a guest speaker at Marshall University in Huntington, West Virginia. At the close of my presentation, I shared with the audience the anecdote about my being crowned fairy princess by my loving family of gay men in San Francisco. When I finished my talk, I received a standing ovation and, coming down off the podium, was immediately surrounded by a large crowd of students and faculty. Some of them pointed out to me that Rhea is the name of a Greek goddess of the earth whose legend has it that she was mother to the great ruling gods of Mount Olympus. I do indeed take my motherly role very seriously, but being compared to a goddess seemed to be stretching things a bit.

The warmth and love extended to me by this particular audience brought on an emotional response that threatened to overpower me. One young man told me that his mother had died just three weeks earlier. Tragically, though he searched his heart, he discovered he had no feeling of loss. She had already died emotionally for him years earlier when he had sought her love and understanding as he struggled to come out to her. Instead, for the remainder of her life she had cruelly rejected him. He told me of how often he had longed for a mother like me, one who could love, accept and respect him just the way he was. It was more than I could bear, and tears of empathetic compassion overflowed my eyes and streamed down my face. For days afterwards the thought of this crowd, and that one young man in particular, again brought tears to my eyes.

A week or so later, just as I had almost recovered from this emotional overload, a package arrived. When I opened it, I once again burst into tears. My husband and son rushed into the room to find out what was the matter. I showed them the note that came with the parcel, it read:

Dear Rhea:

Thank you so much for coming to Huntington and sharing your personal story with us. It was one of the most wonderful presentations I had ever heard. I was very moved by your family's experience.

Only a true blue-blooded princess could conquer hate and ignorance with the loving care and advice you bring by bravely sharing your unique story.

Enclosed is a real rhinestone tiara, necklace and scepter to remember your visit to Magic Makers Costumes. You will meet a lot of wonderful people and make a lot of friends by sharing your life experience. God bless you and know we are always your friends and "at your royal service."

Much admiration,

Ken Fox and Ken Epperly,
Magic Makers Costumes,
Huntington, West Virginia

*

*   *

Today, I find myself a woman characterized by two polar extremes, depending upon who is doing the characterizing. There appears to be absolutely no middle ground. I either represent the Antichrist or the very face of Christ Himself. I am the repudiation of all family values or the embodiment of those values, hopelessly misguided or an undaunted leader, ridiculed or admired, someone to be feared and despised or loved, esteemed and emulated. It is sometimes difficult to maintain my equilibrium, buffeted, as I am, between these two opposing sides. In reality,

I'm quite a plain and ordinary person who loves her gay son without reservation, as all parents should love their children. It's really as simple as that.

Try as I might, it is difficult for me to envision, with any degree of sharp clarity, what the future may hold for me and my family. Four years ago, had someone foretold that we would stand where we do today, I surely would have considered her quite a lunatic and might well have laughed in her face. In truth, I hope the day will arrive, within my lifetime, when it will no longer be necessary for stories like mine to be told, indeed when stories like mine will no longer even happen. I yearn for the day when the mere notion that a precious newborn baby might be gay or lesbian does not strike sheer terror in the hearts of its parents. Like all truly decent people of conscience, I await a time when intolerance, ignorance and prejudice no longer rob mothers and fathers of their parental right to take full delight in their children, regardless of a child's sexual orientation. For we believe all children should be celebrated and rejoiced in, and none should be cast aside, especially not for simply being who they are.

As long as innocent gay and lesbian children continue to be abandoned by their own families, as long as self-affirming gay and lesbian Americans, no matter how capable or gifted, are expected to live in the shadows on the margins of our society, as long as lesbian and gay students are brutalized in high schools everywhere, as long as AIDS patients continue to die needlessly, and while the church continues to deny inclusion at the Lord's table on the basis of a person's sexual orientation, I know I can not remain silent. That true voice of grace and human decency, which dwells deep within the recesses of my soul, would never permit it.

If I could in fact see what the future holds, I'm certain it would overwhelm me. I can only handle it step by step, one day at a time. I am not a courageous woman, but I am a dedicated one. If the past is any indication of the future, all I can know for certain is that fear will be my constant companion. He is with me every time I mount the podium to address another university class or PFLAG chapter, and every time I see a pair of headlights come up too fast behind me on a lonely highway late at night. Fear has become my fellow traveler, and I have learned to accept him as such. But he must settle for being a silent partner. For I will never surrender to him my voice.

Now, when I kneel to take communion before the altar of my tiny Episcopal church, bathed in the sun that streams in through a skylight overhead, many thoughts from the past come rushing into my mind. I think of another altar, the one that stood on the road to my personal Moriah. How dreadfully mistaken I was to ever consider that God would require me to lay my son upon that stone-cold slab, there to sacrifice him to the religious, moral and social conventions of mankind, bound by the shackles of conformity, the heart of his unique human identity impaled upon a dagger of phobic hatred.

Desperately trapped, as I was, between devotion to my church and love for my child, the church offered me an escape hatch by providing a vision of God's love as somehow being conditional. As a mother, therefore, my love for my son might also become conditional, thus releasing me from any responsibility to learn, trust, understand and accept his singular human nature. Agonizing with every step, I groped my way through the dismal emotional wilderness of this dilemma. Eventually, through faith in God, I was led to the reflecting pool of my own soul. In that mirror I saw the face of a woman who had always been driven by her dread of what others might think, a flat, two-dimensional person who had no sense of self, a lonely creature who had never embraced humanity, not even her own. I was that woman.

Then, and only then, was I able to see that it was I, myself, who was bound hand and foot. I was the one immobilized by the powerful cords of conformity and fear, stretched out upon an altar of my own creation. This was the altar to what I saw as the unendurable truth of my child's homosexuality. The dagger was raised above me. I trembled in mortal terror. But, with a graceful, loving hand, God gently guided the knife as it severed those tyrannous cords and set me free.

This book was composed in ITC Bookman and designed by Brown Composition Systems, Inc., Bloomington, Indiana.

Cover design by Melisa Pool. Front cover photography by David Edelfelt. Back cover photography by Butch Murray.

Produced by Gary Pool.